Monday's Child
is Fair of Face

Monday's Child is Fair of Face

. . . and other traditional beliefs about babies and motherhood

Steve Roud

BOOKS

Published by Random House Books 2008

2 4 6 8 10 9 7 5 3 1

Copyright © Steve Roud 2008

Steve Roud has asserted his right under the Copyright, Designs
and Patents Act 1988 to be identified as the author of this work

First published in Great Britain in 2008 by
Random House Books

Random House Books
Random House, 20 Vauxhall Bridge Road,
London SW1V 2SA

www.rbooks.co.uk

Addresses for companies within The Random House Group Limited can be found at:
www.randomhouse.co.uk/offices.htm

The Random House Group Limited Reg. No. 954009

A CIP catalogue record for this book
is available from the British Library

ISBN 9781905211524

The Random House Group Limited supports The Forest Stewardship
Council (FSC), the leading international forest certification organisation.
All our titles that are printed on Greenpeace approved FSC certified paper
carry the FSC logo. Our paper procurement policy can be found at
www.rbooks.co.uk/environment

Typeset by SX Composing DTP, Rayleigh, Essex
Printed and bound by
GGP Media GmbH, Pößneck, Germany

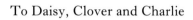
To Daisy, Clover and Charlie

Contents

Babycare

The First Year

Introduction

This is a book about the superstitions and traditions surrounding pregnancy and childbirth in Britain, past and present. It's difficult to define 'superstition', but I think it's best thought of as a belief or custom based on irrational fear of the power of luck and other supernatural forces. It thrives on uncertainty and the feeling of not being in control – childbirth was such a risky business for so many centuries that it attracted more than its fair share of strange notions and beliefs.

Before the days of comprehensive health-care, pregnant women were left largely to their own devices, and most deliveries were in the hands of a local midwife. Indeed, a successful birth relied so much on advice and assistance from mothers and older female acquaintances, that the term 'old wives' tale' is, in this context at least, quite appropriate.

But times have certainly changed. We now have machines which scan, weigh, measure, test and monitor both mother and baby. We have professionally trained personnel, drugs, surgical techniques and a vast knowledge of potential problems and how to deal with them. Similar changes have taken place in many other aspects of life, and so much risk has been taken out of our daily lives that it is no surprise that, as a nation, we are infinitely less superstitious than we used to be. Changes in the basic technology of everyday existence have also done many traditional beliefs to death; there were dozens of superstitious about open fires and candles, but there are none about radiators and light-bulbs; beliefs about horses haven't translated into beliefs about cars; and so on. If we are ill, most of us go to the local doctor, not the local witch-doctor.

Nevertheless, having a baby is still a remarkable event, and there seems to be sufficient mystery involved for 'luck' to play its part. Some superstitious feelings, such as the fear of 'tempting fate', run so deep that we are not always aware of them, and it is unlikely that any new parents-to-be can claim to be completely free of superstition.

As well as looking at superstitions, I've collected together several 'traditional practices' around motherhood and babies. It is astonishing how deeply rooted many of these traditions still are, although they are not all very old. Dressing the baby in pink or blue, for example, is one of the customs firmly embedded in our society, and it has tremendous force behind it. Many people follow the rule unthinkingly, while others are appalled by the implicit gender stereotyping and try to ignore it – not at all easy when all the clothing shops and catalogues are organised on colour/gender lines. But even those who are happy to defy convention and dress their girls in blue would hesitate to send their boys to school in pink! Nevertheless, traditions like these are not fixed forever but come and go over time. Until the early twentieth century, for example, it was quite normal to clothe little boys in dresses, up to the age of four or five.

Some people like to bemoan the fact that we're far less superstitious than our ancestors, rather than welcome it. Old superstitions can seem quaint and romantic – a necessary relief in a world of so much science and technology. But this is only possible now that superstition has lost most of its power and become largely a game. Real superstitious belief is not fun but psychologically crippling, and a world dominated by it is a frightening place. There were a huge number of superstitions based on the idea that women, especially pregnant ones, were naturally unlucky, unreliable, and potentially dangerous to society. Sick people, including newborn babies, could undergo the ministrations of a charmer instead of a doctor or, worse still, be 'doctored' with all manner of plants or other substances.

Nowadays, most people are aware of a few superstitions, but they don't live by them. If they end up doing the 'wrong' thing, the worst they expect is a bit of bad luck, whereas in the past, the penalties were more specific, and more horrific. Less than a hundred years ago, there was a particular notion that if a bride and groom did a certain thing their first baby would be born deaf and blind, and there were numerous superstitions which stated that if such-and-such happened to a pregnant woman, the baby, or the mother, would die within a year. This is far too grim to tell a young expectant mother nowadays.

So, perhaps, we have the best of both worlds. If we really want to know the sex of the baby, we can have a scan, but it does no harm to try a wedding ring suspended on a thread over the mum's abdomen, just for fun. And we don't believe that cats deliberately 'suck the breath' out of a baby, but we know that pet hairs can be harmful to an infant's breathing.

One more thing to bear in mind is that, contrary to popular opinion, superstitions aren't always very old. There is rarely any evidence that a particular superstition goes back to 'pagan times', and many can be shown to be little more than a hundred years old. The fear of Friday the Thirteenth, for example, was invented in Victorian times, and the rhyme *Ring a Ring a Roses* has nothing to do with the plague.

If you want to delve further into the world of superstition you might want to have a look at my *Penguin Dictionary of Superstitions of Britain and Ireland* (2003) or the *Dictionary of Superstitions* by Iona Opie and Moira Tatem (Oxford, 1989). But I hope you find this little book of traditions and superstitions around motherhood and babies an enjoyable place to start.

Where Do Babies Come From?

Two children, on being awakened one morning and informed of
the advent of a new brother, were keen to know whence and how
he arrived. 'It must have been the milkman,' said the girl.
'Why the milkman?' asked her little brother.
'Because he says on his cart "Families supplied".'
Notes & Queries, 1918

Brought or Found

If you buy a baby-announcement card or a congratulations card to send to new parents, the chances are that it will include a picture of a stork. A stork carrying a baby in its beak is one of the instantly recognisable icons of our age, and we all understand its meaning in both pictures and in everyday speech. But the baby-bringing stork is a relatively recent interloper into British folklore, probably little more than about seventy years old, and there were already many other traditional explanations for where babies came from in circulation.

IN THE DOCTOR'S BAG

Adults in previous generations were extraordinarily reluctant to talk openly about birth and babies amongst themselves, let alone in front of children. It may seem strange to us now, but even children brought up in rural areas, surrounded by animals and often living in such crowded conditions that privacy and personal space were a luxury, remained genuinely ignorant of the facts of life. Many children remained entirely unaware of where babies really came from right into their teens. Many were told that the doctor had brought the new infant in his bag, or the nurse in her basket:

> The baby was there when we got home. My mother told me the doctor brought the baby in his black bag. After that I used to watch out for Dr Dwyer and follow him to a house, then run home to tell mum who he had taken a baby to. It was a long time till I found out.
>
> *Northamptonshire Within Living Memory* 1992

UNDER THE GOOSEBERRY BUSHES

Before the advent of the stork, the traditional source of babies was somewhere in the garden – 'under a gooseberry bush' was very common, although other plants, such as currant bushes, were also cited. In Guernsey, for example, babies were found, *sous les caboches*, in the cabbage patch, although they were sometimes brought over in bandboxes from England, in the mail packet:

> Even at the age of fourteen, mother told me she was absolutely convinced that babies grew on gooseberry bushes. Families were kept in complete ignorance about

subjects that didn't, or shouldn't, concern them . . . As Hilda and younger sister Ella were sauntering up the garden path from school one afternoon, a neighbour was knocking urgently at their front door. 'Mrs — is having another B-A-B-Y', she announced. Flustered, their mother ushered them inside, then, spelling the word out, said to the bearer of the news, 'Another B-A-B-Y?' Hilda and Ella could not help wondering about all this secrecy. After all, they did know how to spell. Why another baby from under a gooseberry bush should be such a closely guarded secret they could not understand . . .

Yorkshire, 1915

The garden image was often extended to include suitable corroborative details, such as 'the doctor dug it up with a golden spade', or it was carefully 'dug up, wrapped in a white cloth, and brought into the house when nobody was looking'. Some parents claimed a gender difference: boys were found in the nettles, girls in the parsley bed.

CARRIED BY A STORK

It is strange that even though the stork is such an important part of baby lore in the British Isles, the bird is not even native to these shores. Indeed, it is extremely difficult to pin down exactly when it became naturalised as a genuine part of British lore. Various correspondents addressed the topic in the journal *Notes & Queries* between the 1890s and the 1930s, and they all took it for granted that the stork was part of Dutch and German folklore, but virtually unknown in Britain. We can be sure, however, that at least some of the attributes of the stork in European folklore were already known to British people through the translations of Hans Christian Andersen's stories, which were published in 1846.

By the 1930s, British writers were beginning to refer to the stork without commenting on its foreign provenance, and by the 1950s there is no doubt that the image of the stork was well established:

> The aircraft carrier HMS *Warrior* docked at Devonport on 15 December 1954, with three storks carrying babies painted on the scoreboard on her funnel. The babies were born as the *Warrior* carried refugees to Vietnam. The *Daily Herald* of December 16 had a large illustration of the scoreboard stork-paintings.

Falling Pregnant

Over the centuries, countless notions sought to explain how and why women became pregnant and offered advice to those who wanted to conceive. These ranged from having sex while the tide was coming in or at the time of the full moon to encouraging nature by eating special diets:

> Fen handywomen distilled a mandrake tea which they dispensed to childless wives who longed to become mothers.

> Cambridgeshire, 1969

'CATCHING' A PREGNANCY

Many childbirth beliefs involve a strong element of 'contagious magic', whereby pregnancy is treated as if it is catching. It is often said that women of child-bearing age should avoid sitting on a chair just vacated by someone who is pregnant, and there have been many variations on the same idea.

> Many women believed that if you sat down on a mother's bed to look at the new baby, you would be the next woman in the street to have one.
>
> Lincoln, 1930s

> A barren woman is often told chaffingly to 'tak' a rub' against a pregnant woman and 'get some o' her luck'.
>
> Fife fishing community, 1912

With so many opportunities to fall pregnant by accident, it's not hard to see why measures were sometimes required to prevent it happening:

> If you are in the company of two pregnant women slap your backside three times or you too will become pregnant.
>
> County Tyrone, 1972

Sometimes the pregnancy was thought to be transmitted by more indirect means:

Should two women pour tea from the same brewing, one of them would have a baby within the year, or a member of that woman's family would have a new arrival. The same is said should your apron drop from your waist.

Wiltshire, 1975

A man and woman may not dry their hands on the same towel after washing, and a woman may not pour out tea or any drink in another woman's house, especially after the hostess has started doing so. In both cases the woman would become pregnant.

Cambridgeshire, 1939

And it wasn't just a mother who was able to transmit pregnancy to other young women. Babies too were thought to have certain powers:

If a baby looks at you from between its legs you will get pregnant.

Sheffield, 1982

RUM BUTTER

Traditionally, family and friends would gather together immediately after a birth to celebrate the new arrival. Rum butter would often be served, and it was thought to have many beneficial qualities for both children and adults, not least of which was helping women to conceive:

There seems to have been some idea that rum butter was an aid to fertility, especially when eaten by married women, and it was thought to be more efficacious when made for the birth of a boy than when for a girl.

Cumberland, 1929

HERBS AND PLANTS

Over the years, numerous plants have been thought to play a particular role in the process of becoming and remaining pregnant. A contributor to Roy Vickery's *Dictionary of Plant-Lore* (1995), for example, reported a belief about the plant *Arum maculatum* (often called Lords and Ladies, or Cuckoo Pint):

When we were very young at school (and innocent) we used to say you should never touch a *cuckoo pint*; if you did you'd become pregnant.

Dorset, 1982

Vickery suggests that the flower's phallus-shaped spadix might have suggested this interpretation. The cuckoo pint was, however, only one of many plants credited with similar powers:

The seed of docks tied to the left arm of a woman will prevent her being barren.

Ireland, 1888

Seaweed was also thought to have special powers, although as this story related by A. T. Culloty in his book *Drinking from the Well* (1993) shows, some people remained sceptical about its effects:

There were two farmers from the richer side of Duhallow, the eastern side, *a bhuachaill* [my boy]. They were a distance apart, but usually met at the fairs in Newmarket and would retire for a little *taoscán* [a small measure of drink] together. Now, they both had good farms of land, were both married, but, *mo bhrón* [sadly], neither of them had a family. As usual at that time the wives were blamed.

Now, this day they met again at Newmarket Fair, and retired for sustenance. In the course of conversation Dan said to Jack, 'I hear that Ballybunion [seaweed baths] is a great place to send the women. There is great good in them baths back there.' Jack listened but didn't reply. Dan sent the wife to Ballybunion and fair enough, in due time they were blessed with a fine bouncing son. Some time later, at a fair, again in Newmarket, Dan and Jack met and fell to talking over refreshments in the bar. In the course of the conversation Dan announced the good news. That gave excuse for a few more drinks and when they finally emerged they took some time to say their good-byes. Before parting, Dan slapped Jack on the shoulder and with a shouted whisper said, 'I would strongly advise you to send your wife to Ballybunion.' 'I

London Bridge is Falling Down

> London Bridge is falling down,
> Falling down, falling down,
> London Bridge is falling down,
> My fair lady.

The two ingredients for a great nursery rhyme are a delightful tune and simple, mysterious, imaginative words, and *London Bridge* amply fulfils all these criteria. We all know the first verse, but few of us nowadays go through the whole story (each verse constructed in the same way as the first):

> Build it up with wood and clay . . .
> Wood and clay will wash away . . .
> Build it up with bricks and mortar . . .
> Bricks and mortar will not stay . . .
> Build it up with iron and steel . . .
> Iron and steel will bend and bow . . .
> Build it up with silver and gold . . .
> Silver and gold will be stolen away . . .
> Set a man to watch all night . . .
> Suppose the man should fall asleep . . .
> Give him a pipe to smoke all night . . .

It is perhaps the oldest of the rhymes still in the active nursery repertoire, although the earliest concrete reference in English only dates from 1620. There are many close parallels across Europe of bridges falling and bridges repaired, some of which are older than ours, but it is impossible to know now which came first.

The Pregnancy

'Hard Cheese – it's Son No. 6!'

Mum Denise Long was a bit cheesed off yesterday when she
discovered she had given birth to a boy – her sixth son. Blonde
Denise had been on a special dairy diet during pregnancy which
was meant to guarantee a girl, according to old wives' tales. 'I was
mad for cheese the whole time I was pregnant and really thought it
would be a girl this time after five boys,' said the 33-year-old mum
yesterday . . .

Daily Mirror, 9 April 1986

Tips For a Successful Pregnancy

Once a woman became pregnant, she was immediately subject to a wide range of prohibitions and restrictions on her actions, which were mostly based on the idea that whatever she did could affect the baby, both physically and psychologically. The firm belief in these antenatal influences was, it seems, universal, and their effects could manifest in various ways, whether as birthmarks and other unusual physical characteristics or as phobias and other mental traumas:

Any fear on the part of the mother, such as the fear of some animals, of thunder, or any objection to things, such as fur, chalk, or certain colours, are believed to be transmissible. A friend of mine has a fear of the sound of flowing water in the dark, although in daylight it causes the contrary sensation. He cannot remember the time when he had not this feeling of dread, but was grown up

before he knew that his grandfather was drowned in a
flooded river through missing his way in the dark.

Wales, 1930

Superstition sought to provide explanations for such seem-
ingly inexplicable feelings or any abnormality in a child's
appearance. In most cases, the event that caused them was
attributed to accident rather than to the behaviour of the
mother-to-be, but there still remained dozens of beliefs that
advised restrictions on a mother-to-be's movements and
activities, and blamed her if things went wrong. Here, for
example, is just one paragraph in a chapter on Welsh birth
folklore, collected by Marie Trevelyan in 1909. It includes
so many prohibitions and warnings that it is a wonder
women in previous times dared do anything at all while
expecting.

[A pregnant woman] must not walk or step over a grave.
If she does her child will die. If she dips her fingers in
dirty water, her child will have coarse hands. If she ties a
cord around her waist, her child will be unlucky. If she
turns the washing-tubs upside down as soon as she has
finished with them, her child will be tidy and orderly. If
she passes through any kind of tangle, her child will have
a life of confusion. If she meddles much with flowers, her
child will not have a keen sense of smell. If she has a great
longing for fish her child will be born too soon, or
will soon die. 'She must not spin,' said people in the

eighteenth century, 'for if she does, flax or hemp will be made into the rope that will hang her child.' If, instead of eating at a table, she goes to the cupboard and 'picks at food', her child will be a glutton. If she dusts furniture with her apron, her child will be very disorderly.

While there seem to have been any number of gloomy predictions and warnings of dire consequences faced by the unwary mother-to-be and her child, there appear to have been very few indeed of the opposite stamp. Whereas it could be quite 'logical', in a symbolic way, for example, to argue that a pregnant woman who spent a lot of time spinning and weaving thus ensured that her baby would be industrious, the superstitious mind said 'no, the baby will die by hanging'. Nobody listed all the good things an expectant parent could do to benefit the baby in the womb.

It is interesting to note how different things are today. Expectant mothers are nowadays exhorted to play Mozart and read to their unborn babies, to help them on the way to being born geniuses. The idea is no less superstitious than those gloomy predictions quoted above, but is infinitely more pleasant to contemplate.

Of the few superstitions that offered the chance of exerting a positive influence upon the unborn child, a fair number involved the use of plants and herbs. Nicholas Culpeper (1616–54), for example, in his famous *Complete Herbal*, recommended sage and tansy to prevent miscarriage, observing of the latter plant that 'the very smell of it stays abortion, or miscarriages in women'. Other plant products that were supposedly useful in preventing miscarriage include conserve of roses, plantain seeds and tormentil roots.

Another group of superstitions stressed the importance of a mother-to-be being allowed to indulge any cravings she might develop during her pregnancy.

AVOID SHOCKS

In the stories invented to explain birthmarks and other unusual characteristics, the sights or events which got the blame were typically things that had frightened or distressed the mother-to-be, the sudden surge in emotion that they caused later affecting the baby's appearance. Kate Mary Edwards, who was born around 1880 and who lived in the Huntingdonshire fens all her life, talked about the subject to her daughter Sybil Marshall, who published her mother's words in her book *Fenland Chronicle* (1967):

> I know all these birthmarks are laughed at nowadays, as old wives tales, but we believed in such things. When I were a child I had a white lock down the back o' my head – where it growed because my mother were frightened by a white bear at Peterborough Fair; another child had a slice of beetroot on his leg, because his mother slapped her leg when fancying a bit o' beetroot, and another one a bunch o' fly-blows on her nose 'cos her mother pinched her nose when she found a bit o' meat fly-blowed and

stinking. Then there's a man with a pair of greyhounds leaping up his back, and another with black pig-skin and bristles on his head, because his mother looked at a black pig what had burned to death in a fire.

In most communities it was considered everyone's responsibility to protect expectant mothers from these dangers and pains were taken to shield pregnant women from distressing sights and situations.

The belief in maternal impressions is of course fixed and certain; and wonderful are the tales told of children born with a 'snap' on the cheek (through the favourite piece of confectionery having been playfully thrown at the mother) or with a mouse on the leg, e.g. a woman who was slapped in the face with a red handkerchief while pregnant, had a child with a red mark on the forehead; another woman had a 'red hand' on her own abdomen because before her birth her mother's night-gown caught fire, and she had laid her hand violently on her body to extinguish the flames. It is always considered among the folk a most reprehensible thing to throw anything, even in jest, at a pregnant woman, on account of thereby causing a birthmark, or even a marked deformity, to the future offspring. Should something be thrown, however, and the part hit be an uncovered part of the body, such as the face, neck, or hand, the probable birthmark may be transferred to a part covered with clothes, if the woman touches with her hand the spot where she has been struck, and then touches a clothed part of her person. A young married woman is always so advised by her elders. The transference is only effectual before the fourth month of pregnancy. Any start or fright to a pregnant woman is considered dangerous, as the child may 'put up its hand and grip the mother's heart'. I have heard sudden death in pregnancy attributed to this.

Fife fishing community, 1912

Birthmarks and other 'defects' were mostly seen as the simple result of occurrences during pregnancy, but the belief in prenatal influence sometimes had deeper implications. Marks could, for example, be interpreted as indicating the future for the baby:

Red birth-marks round the neck of a child are called the 'hangman's sign', and he will come to the gallows.

Wales, 1909

AVOID HARES

One of the best-known examples of belief in antenatal influence was the cleft palate, *cheiloschisis*, almost universally known as a 'harelip'. This was caused by a pregnant woman meeting a hare, and could only be counteracted by swift action on the part of the woman, who was advised immediately to tear a few inches off the bottom of her dress or petticoat. As early as the sixteenth century, pregnant women were being advised to leave a small piece of their dress unstitched, just in case they needed to tear it in a hurry.

There were numerous variations on the theme. It was reported in County Cavan, for example, that pregnant women were also in danger from dead hares being carried home by huntsmen. The dead animal could be rendered safe, however, if the tail was removed, and men were regarded as grossly irresponsible if they neglected to take this elementary precaution in case they met an expectant mother on their way home. The harelip belief dates back at least to the mid-sixteenth century, and was still being quoted in the mid-twentieth century. It was given a boost by a bestselling novel by Mary Webb, published in 1924, in which the main character suffered from this affliction, as mentioned in the autobiography of socialite celebrity Lady Diana Cooper (née Manners), who was expecting a baby in 1929:

Our seaside haven was still unravished, and there we retired from worldly labours . . . to marvel and dream about my child, very happy though a little apprehensive, marking auguries and omens. A sitting hare would not get out of the way of our car. This to one who had read Mary Webb's *Precious Bane*, augured a hare-lip for my baby.

AVOID LIONS

By definition, superstitions are irrational beliefs and operate on a different level to 'normal' ways of thought, but it is usually possible to discern some form of underlying 'logic' when they are analysed, compared and contrasted. Some, however, are so bizarre that they defy any attempt at understanding or explanation, and all one can say is 'how on earth did people believe that?' Into this category falls a pair of beliefs which presume an intimate connection between lions and pregnant women. In the first, it is claimed that the breeding cycle of lions – strangely set at seven years – affects the breeding of humans and other animals:

> 'It's a very bad year for the women this year.' 'Indeed – why so?' 'Why, ma'am, it's the seventh year, the year the lioness has her young, and it's sure to be a bad time with the women then.'
>
> Shropshire, 1883

This belief was also recorded in various other parts of the country from the 1870s onwards and was still current in the 1950s. Occasionally, the animal in question was an elephant or a bear, but in the majority of cases it was a lion.

The second lion-related belief current about the same period claimed that lions cannot bear to be in the presence of pregnant humans. Kate Edwards provided a graphic description of this notion, published in her daughter Sybil

Marshall's *Fenland Chronicle*. The author records her mother's memory of the visit of a travelling menagerie, or 'wild beast show', to the neighbourhood, about 1890:

It warn't a circus – there were no performing animals. It were just a chance for country folk to see the queer creatures. They had a big tent and inside all the cages were set so as you could walk round and look at them. Outside the main door there was allus a big fire a-burning, with great long iron rods, red hot in it. These were to control the animals if they got excited and out of hand. One year when the show were on at Ramsey there were quite a bit of excitement. The lions suddenly started to git so troublesome that it seemed they'd break out o' their cages. They roared and snarled and pounded their bars, that the men had to come a-running with their red-hot bars, but even then they couldn't quieten them.

Then the manager came out and announced that he would have to ask the lady who was expecting a child, who was in the tent, to leave. He said 'e knowed what the matter was, because lions could allus smell a woman as was expecting, and then they allus behaved like this, though he ha'n't ever knowed 'em to be so bad before.

Well there was a poor young woman there as were like to have a child soon. When she found the lions a-roaring at her and everybody a-blaming her and pushing her outside the tent, she were so frightened and upset that she fainted right away. I remember my mother and her neighbours a-talking about it, and if I remember aright, they blamed her a bit for ever going to a wild beast show in such a state. Of course, they thought such an experience would mark the child, and that it 'ould be born with a lion's mane or something like that.

This idea is clearly allied to an incident included in Tobias Smollett's novel *Humphry Clinker* (1771), in which it is stated that lions always go wild if approached by a young woman who 'is not a maiden'. What the basis of these beliefs was is anybody's guess.

GIVE IN TO CRAVINGS

It was widely believed that unborn babies would be adversely affected if their mothers' cravings for particular foods were not satisfied. Some people nowadays believe that cravings are nature's way of warning the mother that she needs certain vitamins or minerals, while others reckon it is nature having a little joke, but either way there is no denying their power.

Cravings are not simply a phenomenon of the modern affluent society, but have been recorded in all periods. Kate Edwards, in the *Fenland Chronicle* again:

Everybody as were expecting 'ould have 'fancies', usually fancying something they couldn't get. Then when the child were born it 'ould be buttoning up its mouth and licking its lips, and the old women 'ould say:

'He wants as little bit of whatever it were yew fancied.
What warrit?' And if it were possible, they'd rub the
baby's mouth with whatever it was, like a sour apple or a
pickled onion, or whatever and say 'Now it'll be
satisfied.' I'm heard my mother say that the first thing as
ever passed my lips were a tiny bit of hare's brain.

Silas Todd, of London, recorded an unfortunate incident in
his autobiography, first published in 1786, in which the loss
of a baby was blamed on the mother's failure to get what she
'craved':

One evening, as my wife was occasionally at her
accustomed chandler's shop . . . she discovered a leg of
pork roasting by the fire, and being big with her fourth
child, longed for to eat of it. Mr C. was ever free with our
family in what my house afforded; therefore my wife
naturally imagined a similar degree of freedom on her
part would not be considered as an act of rudeness by Mr
C. . . . [He, however, refused her. She] went home and
informed her mother of the illiberality of Mr C., who
went immediately to him and related to him my wife's
condition; upon which he raved, swore, and replied,
'What can I not have a joint of meat, but she must long
for it?' Her mother, struck with his behaviour, quickly
informed me thereof. I then went round to him myself,
and offered him half a guinea for a plate-ful of the pork,
which he sharply refused. This broke off, for ever

afterwards, our acquaintance; but I do not imagine that the disappointment would have affected my wife, had it not been principally owing to the weakness of her mother, who informed her of the man's cruel behaviour; which was so heavy an effect on her, that the child became emaciated within her, insomuch as she was never delivered but lay eight months under the physician's care.

One further example can be given, from the *Shrewsbury Chronicle* (8 November 1811), although here it is impossible to know whether the husband was telling the whole truth:

A poor man was convicted before the magistrates at Lewes [Sussex], in the penalty of £5, for shooting a hare. On saying he was unable to pay the fine, he was asked if he had any household furniture, to which he replied he had six small children, and that to satisfy the longings of a pregnant wife and to prevent the deformity of the child, he had ventured to trespass by shooting the hare.

Boy or Girl?

Before the days of scans and tests, the big question in everybody's mind was 'Will it be a boy or a girl?', and it is hardly surprising that there was a bewildering array of infallible signs which could be brought to bear on the problem of prediction. A selection from those given by Mary Chamberlain in her book *Old Wives' Tales* (1981) provides a good sample:

Heartburn means a girl.
Take bicarbonate of soda to ensure a boy child.
If you long for sweet foods during pregnancy you will have a girl, if you long for sour things, a boy.
If you don't feel much movement from the baby it's a boy.
Nausea early in pregnancy means it will be a girl.
If the baby's late it will be a boy.

Another list, from De Garis's book of *Guernsey Folklore* (1975) shows some overlap:

> If the expectant mother suffers from heartburn the baby will be a girl.
> It is also thought to be a girl if the mother carries the child to the front.
> If she carries 'all round', it will be a boy.
> A baby that is overdue is expected to be a boy.

Hundreds of other infallible signs have been quoted to prospective parents throughout the British Isles over the centuries. The beauty of these predictions, of course, is that they have a good chance of being right at least half the time, and those are pretty good odds for any prophecy.

THE 'PENDULUM TEST'

One 'sure-fire' method that is still carried out in fun by many mums-to-be is the old pendulum test:

> Women would also try to determine the sex by moving needle and cotton as a pendulum over the pregnant woman's abdomen. If it circles, it's a girl; if it sways to and fro, a boy.
>
> Lincolnshire, 1992

Unfortunately, there is little agreement about the meaning, as some sources say that a circle means a boy and a straight line a girl. Many versions stipulate a wedding ring as the item suspended. The idea that a pendulum can reveal hidden secrets, or help to choose between different courses of action, is first mentioned in Britain in the 1580s, although its use in guessing a baby's sex cannot be proven to be older than the early twentieth century.

HOW THE BABY WAS CONCEIVED

It seems that parents often turned to the point of conception to provide information about the baby. Here's a rather magical method for determining the sex of the child:

> Some time ago I was told by a woman . . . that at the birth of a child the phase of the moon should be noted, as by that it was possible to foretell the sex of the next child. She went on to say that a lady living near would have a son born soon, and another neighbour would have a daughter – 'I know, for I looked at the moon when their last children were born,' she said. I must add that when the babies arrived they proved to be as she had prophesied.
>
> Guernsey, 1915

And here's a slightly more down-to-earth method:

> Children (generally illegitimate) 'gotten oot o' doors'
> were expected to be boys. 'It couldna but be a laddie, it
> was gotten amang the green grass.'
>
> Fife fishing community, 1912

NUMEROLOGY

Great fun can be had assigning numerical values to letters and
working out complicated calculations to predict the future. In
the *Royal Dream Book and Fortune Teller*, published about
1860 but reprinted numerous times since, the following
advice was given to expectant parents:

> To know if a woman with child will have a girl or boy:
> Write the proper names of the father and the mother, and
> of the month she conceived with child, and likewise
> adding all the numbers of those letters [A=1, B=2, etc.]
> together, divide them by seven; and then, if the
> remainder be even, it will be a girl, if uneven it will be a
> boy.

OLDER SIBLINGS

Prediction does not stop once the baby is born, because it is
the new little one's responsibility to announce the sex of the
next in line:

If an infant learns to say 'dada' first, the next child will be a boy; if it says 'mam' first the next child will be a girl.

Wales, 1909

If the child's first cry can be twisted into 'dey' (father), the next comer will be a male.

Fife fishing community, 1912

Ring a Ring a Roses

Ring a ring a roses,
A pocket full of posies,
A-tishoo! a-tishoo!
We all fall down.

Ring a Roses is nowadays one of the first singing games which parents teach their children, and in some form or other it has been popular all over the English-speaking world for about 130 years. The modern words vary little, but in the past there were considerable differences between versions which make it difficult to estimate how the words might have been in the original. One of the earliest versions noted in Britain, for example, was published in Kate Greenaway's *Mother Goose* in 1881:

Ring-a-ring-a-roses
A pocket full of posies
Hush! hush! hush! hush!
We're all tumbled down.

And two other versions from the following decade show something of the range of variability at the time:

> Ring a ring o' roses
> A pocket-full o' posies
> One for me, one for you
> And one for little Moses.
> Hasher, Hasher, Hasher, all fall down.
>
> Lincolnshire, c. 1894

> Ring a ring a row-o
> See the children go-o
> Sit below the goose-berry bush
> Hark! they all cry Hush! hush! hush!
> Sitty down, sit down.

> Duzzy duzzy gander
> Sugar, milk and candy
> Hatch-u, hatch-u, all fall down together.
>
> South Shields, c. 1894

A comparison of all the early versions shows that it is possible that the original text did not include sneezing, but 'hushing', and that the 'falling down' was originally curtseying or bowing, rather than falling.

But some time in the middle of the twentieth century, probably in the 1940s, somebody had the bright idea that the rhyme describes the plague, and dates from the time of the Great Plague of 1666. Despite being complete nonsense, this idea, after simmering for a while, spread like wildfire in the 1960s, and it is no exaggeration to say that the vast majority of people now believe it without question. Attempts to correct people on the matter are often met with disbelief and even anger, as many people object to the destruction of romantic legend by the cold water of fact. But the plague theory rests on the flimsiest of evidence, and the case against it is very strong. The first known versions are more than two hundred years after the Great Plague; no writer at the time of the plague, or after, mentions it; earlier collectors of children's rhymes do not include it; sneezing and red patches are not symptoms of the plague, and so on. In summary, the rhyme did not exist, and the internal details which are said to corroborate the theory are completely wrong. It is almost certain that the whole idea was constructed by somebody who latched onto the 'posies' detail and extrapolated from the idea that people in the past carried nosegays to prevent infection in times of sickness.

Small children, however, are right not to care about such things, as they simply enjoy the tune and the actions. Not very long ago, some playgroup teacher or other organiser of children's games hit on an idea of how to extend the fun and get the children back up:

> Cows in the meadow
> Eating butter cups,
> One two three
> And we all jump up.

or alternatively

> Picking up the daisies,
> Picking up the daisies,
> A-tishoo, a-tishoo!
> We all jump up.

These may lack some of the poetry and mystery of the earlier versions, but the children love them.

The Birth

A Charm to Release a Woman in Travell: Throw over the top of the house, where a woman in travell lieth, a stone, or any other thing that hath killed three living creatures; namely, a man, a wild boar, and a she-bear.

Reginald Scot, *Discoverie of Witchcraft*, 1584

Giving Birth

It is hardly surprising that something as unpredictable and potentially dangerous as childbirth should have inspired a multitude of magical and superstitious practices over the years. Many of these practices were well known in their time, and were believed as implicitly as modern scientific methods are, although they appear bizarre to modern eyes. Nevertheless, despite their apparent outlandishness, the underlying principles are often very simple.

As with other areas of daily life, there were many who put their faith in verbal charms – words which when recited in the correct way at the correct time were deemed to have a powerful effect. These charms were invariably couched in Christian terms, and there is little to distinguish them from prayers. A more overtly magical procedure, which was extremely widespread in various forms, was to tie a particular item around the mother's waist or thigh, with the magic residing in the item itself and its position on the body. A third range of procedures was based on the relatively simple symbolic action of unlocking or unblocking items in the immediate vicinity of the childbed, in the belief that the baby's passage would be similarly eased. Another category encompassed belief in amulets or inanimate objects imbued with magical power of their own, and effective merely by their presence at the scene. Two very different but widespread examples of these amulets are the eagle-stone and the printed 'Saviour's Letter' broadsides.

THE POWER OF CHARMS

The idea of placing something around the expectant mother's waist, or thigh, was popular from at least the fifteenth century and was widely familiar until the eighteenth century. A wide range of items was used, and they were generally referred to as 'girdles', each with some sort of semi-religious or magical association to give it power. Many had religious writings on them invoking the aid of St Margaret or the Virgin Mary, but others gained their power from previous association. Bessie Dunlop, who was accused of witchcraft in Scotland in 1576, spoke at her interrogation of a piece of lace obtained from the fairies, which was used to ease delivery. Other accounts mention pieces of string that had been used to measure the height of a saint, or simply cut to the exact height of Jesus Christ, while others used a piece of rope from a church bell, and so on. The basic principle was still in operation in late Victorian times:

In a Hampshire village until a recent date, if not at the present time, a piece of red tape was tied round one of the thighs of a woman in child-bed, as it was supposed to mitigate the labour-pains and to prevent any mishap.

1898

Other charms could be worked with a piece of string or lace, as recorded by Reginald Scot in his *Discoverie of Witchcraft*:

Women with child run to church and tie their girdles or shoe latchets [laces] about a bell, and strike upon the same thrice, thinking that the sound thereof hasteth their good delivery.

OPENING DOORS

A superstition that appears to have a very straightforward symbolic meaning is that removing obstacles in the house will ease a difficult birth.

In a prolonged or tedious labour an older woman would often open the door and leave it slightly ajar.

Fife fishing community, 1912

More thoroughly, women in attendance can undo all the locks in the house, including doors, cupboards, boxes, and so on. Interestingly, the same procedure was commonly recommended to ease the passing of anyone dying in the house.

UNCROSSING LEGS

The belief that all women present at the birth should refrain from crossing their legs has a very long history indeed. Spare a thought for poor Alcmene, who, in Ancient Greek legend, was expecting twins by different fathers. One son, Iphicles, was by her husband, Amphitryon, and the other, Heracles (or Hercules), was conceived when the god Zeus visited her, cunningly disguised as her husband. But when her time came, Heracles' birth was deliberately delayed by Zeus' wife Hera (or Juno) out of jealousy:

> When the natal hour of the toil-bearing Hercules was near . . . seven nights and days I was in torture . . . There cruel Juno sat . . . listening to my groans, with her right knee crossed over her left, and with her fingers interlocked; and so she stayed the birth . . . and prevented my deliverance.
>
> Ovid's Metamorphoses, c. AD 8

A similar effect could be achieved by ill-wishers tying knots, with appropriate incantations, during the birth, although this was more usually done at an earlier stage, during the marriage ceremony, as a curse to prevent conception:

> If anyone at a marriage repeats the benediction after the priest, and ties a knot at the mention of each of the three sacred names on a handkerchief, or a piece of string, the

marriage will be childless for fifteen years, unless the knotted string is burnt in the meantime.

County Galway, 1891

In some Scottish reports there was a simple solution: the bridegroom need only leave his shoelaces untied for the duration of the wedding ceremony.

EAGLE-STONES

Of all the birth charms and amulets of the early modern period, the most famous, and perhaps the most curious, was the *aetites*, or 'eagle-stone'. This was a natural formation of iron oxide in which an outer casing enclosed a smaller stone. It is not really surprising that such an apparently 'pregnant' stone should have taken on magical attributes concerned with childbirth, but it was quite versatile. When worn around the neck, or tied to the arm, it was believed to be a powerful protection against miscarriage, but care had to be taken as the actual day of birth approached. If it remained on the upper part of the body when the birth process began, the eagle-stone would prolong labour indefinitely, so at the appropriate moment it had to be transferred to the mother's thigh, where it would function to ease the pangs of birth and ensure a swift and simple delivery.

Yesterday I delivered to your grandmother Legh an Eagle Stone in an Indian silk bag, a paper sew'd upon it, No. 21, and in it a paper wrote upon – 'Eagle stones good to prevent miscarriages of women with child, to be worn about the neck and left off two or three weeks before the reckoning be out.' I had another of them which was smooth, having been polished, which I believe was that which you wrote to your grandmother about. It was lent to Sir Francis Leycester's lady.

So wrote Sir Streynsham Master to his daughter, wife of the Earl of Coventry, in 1716. Eagle-stones are a nice reminder that superstition and 'magical thinking' was not confined to the poor, uneducated, rural population, but was also shared by the richest and most well-educated people in the country. Indeed, it was only members of this class who could afford to obtain an eagle-stone when the need arose, and much of the historical information we possess on the topic is found in surviving letters that refer to them being passed around between friends and family. Clearly, any item that could deliver such a desirable effect would be much sought after, and genuine eagle-stones changed hands for large sums of money. Those who possessed them were constantly asked to lend them: 'It is so useful my wife can seldom keep it at home', wrote the Dean of Christchurch, Canterbury, in 1676, and an advertisement in the *London Gazette* of April 1686 offered a handsome reward for one which had been lost:

An eagle stone tied up in a piece of black ribbon with two long black strings at the end of it, lost the 29th inst.

Broadsides were cheaply printed papers sold in the streets; they contained news, ballads, tales of wonders, last dying speeches of executed criminals, accounts of scandals (real and concocted) and a host of other topics. *A Copy of a Letter Written by Our Saviour Jesus Christ* was in the catalogue of most of the leading broadside printers of the early nineteenth century, and although versions vary a little, it typically contained an interesting mixture of religious items, held together by the idea of a 'letter'. The main section claims to be the text of a letter actually written by Jesus, and 'found under a great stone, round and large, at the foot of the Cross, near a village called Mesopotamia'. It urges followers, at some length, to keep the Sabbath holy and not to work, nor to dress up with 'superfluities of costly apparel and vain dresses, for I have ordained a day of rest'. There follows a list of 'Christ's Cures and Miracles'. The next section comprises the letter from King Agbarus, taken from the *Apocrypha* (the collection of early religious writings which did not make it into the official Bible). In this, the king invites Jesus Christ to his city, firstly to cure the disease from which he is suffering, but also for the Saviour to take shelter there from his enemies. 'Our Saviour's answer' is also given, and says, in effect, 'Thanks, but I'm busy. I'll send you a disciple later on.' The last section on the sheet is a copy of 'Lentulus's Epistle to the Senate of Rome, containing a Description of Jesus Christ'.

The paragraph that really grabbed people's attention and gave the letter its status as a powerful amulet, comes near the end of the main letter:

... and whosoever shall have a copy of this letter, written by my own hand, and keep it in their houses, nothing shall hurt them, neither pestilence, lightning, nor thunder shall do them any hurt. And if a woman be with child, and in labour, and a copy of this letter be about her, and she firmly puts her trust in me, she shall be safely delivered of her birth.

There is no doubt that many ordinary people believed implicitly in the authenticity of the letter and therefore in its efficacy. Many cottages had a copy of the broadside pinned on the wall; alternatively, one was kept reverently folded between the pages of the family Bible, to be brought out when needed.

The Timing of the Birth

The idea that the timing of someone's birth is an important key to their future character and fortune is old and deeply ingrained in British society, as elsewhere. There is no doubt that the bulk of the population has been interested in astrology, in a vague way, since at least the Middle Ages, but it is interesting to see how superficial this interest has always been, and how little it impinged on everyday superstitions and popular beliefs. Cheap annual almanacs, found in most households from the sixteenth to the early twentieth centuries, provided basic astrological information and were read and commented on by all and sundry, but there is little evidence of a systematic or in-depth knowledge among the ordinary people at any time in history, including the present. Serious astrology requires a high level of astronomical knowledge and mathematical ability beyond the scope or interest of most people. Everybody knows their star sign (more accurately called a sun sign) but most are content to leave it at that.

In the range of personal superstitions and beliefs collected by folklorists, astrology is hardly ever mentioned, and the only interest in the position of planetary bodies is a concern about the phases of the moon. But there were many other ways in which the time of birth affected character, and there were plenty of signs ready to be interpreted, operating on various levels, although, curiously enough, by far the most frequent prediction is whether or not the baby will be able to see ghosts or have other extrasensory capabilities. Significance could be found in the time of day a birth took place, the day of the week, the month or season, the phase of the moon or the state of the tide at the time, while some read meaning into other signs, such as weather conditions:

> To be born at night made one open to see visions, ghosts and phantom funerals. A child born during a storm would lead a troublesome life. To be born when the moon is on the increase is a good omen.
>
> Wales, 1930

Naturally enough, any occurrence that general superstition regarded as bad would be interpreted as a negative indication of the baby's character or prospects. So, for example, a wild bird fluttering against the bedroom window, which was seen as extremely unlucky at any time, would inevitably be interpreted as predicting a very short life for the new baby.

LUCKY AND UNLUCKY MONTHS

Many beliefs have circulated about the best time of the year for a birth, but it is very difficult to arrange them in any sort of coherent system. May, for example, was the only month generally singled out for its special significance, and had a baleful reputation. In the modern mind, May is usually seen as a 'good' month, full of the promise of summer and the regeneration of nature, and a time for outdoor rejoicings. But in superstition, May is oddly cast as generally unlucky and not to be trusted. There was an extremely widespread belief, for example, that kittens born in May were weak and if they survived would grow to be useless as cats. This distrust of 'May' animals applied to other species, especially farm animals, and even spilled over into the human sphere. May babies were never expected to thrive or to amount to much in life, and people born in the month would excuse any shortcomings or failures with: 'Well, I'm only a May kitten, you know.' In Derbyshire in 1895 it was agreed that children born in the month of May require great care in bringing up, for 'May chickens come cheeping'.

BIRTHSTONES

One of the mainstays of the jewellery trade, for the last hundred years or so, has been the idea that there is a special stone for each month which is particularly lucky or appropriate for anybody born in that period. The scheme varies a little, but one standard list is as follows:

January – garnet
February – amethyst
March – bloodstone/aquamarine
April – diamond
May – emerald
June – pearl
July – cornelian/ruby
August – sardonyx (a variety of onyx)
September – sapphire
October – opal
November – topaz
December – turquoise

As is the case with many modern popular traditions, the origin of the birthstone scheme is difficult to pin down. While many cultures have long had beliefs about particular stones being magical or protective, it seems that the organisation of these into one for each month, and the idea that these stones were therefore lucky for those born in that period is, in Britain at least, surprisingly recent.

Nearly all writers on the subject state categorically that birthstones are an ancient phenomenon, which may be true in one sense, but the implication that there has been an unbroken tradition for 2000 years 'til the present day is almost certainly false. It is usually claimed that the system originates from the Bible, but the two references normally cited – Exodus 28:15–21 and Revelation 21:19–20 – both refer to twelve precious stones, one for each of the tribes of

Israel, without a hint of 'lucky' stones or birthdays.

But Jewish historians were already moving in the direction of some sort of system in the first century AD. Flavius Josephus (around AD 37–95), for example, wrote:

> As for the twelve stones, whether we understand by them the months, or the signs of what the Greeks call the zodiac, we shall not be mistaken in their meaning.

Enthusiastic European astrologers of later times also took these biblical references and tried to fit them into their zodiac systems: anything divided into twelve was grist to their mill. But there is little indication that the scheme entered into common parlance until much later, and there is a fair amount of negative evidence to suggest that it definitely did not.

In Britain, cheap almanacs of the early nineteenth century, for example, which were deeply concerned with the calendar, signs of the zodiac, predictions, and so on, make no mention of a birthstone scheme, and those antiquarian writers who organised their books around the calendar, such as William Hone's *Every-Day Book* (1827) and Robert Chambers' *Book of Days* (1864), are similarly silent on the matter. Birthstones are similarly conspicuous by their absence in the collections of late-Victorian and Edwardian folklorists in this country.

As we get closer to the twentieth century, however, evidence begins to appear in abundance. The *Sunlight Almanac* (1896) gives a list of stones for each month (unfortunately omitting October), which are as above, except for three: April – sapphire; June – agate; September – chrysolite; but this list does not mention birthdays. By 1902, the idea was definitely beginning to take hold, and there are many references in popular publications such as *Pearson's Fortune Teller*, edited by P. R. S. Foli, which tells us, for instance, that 'an amulet should consist of the stone corresponding to the month in which its possessor was born'.

The evidence so far points to the fact that there was no popular tradition of precious and semi-precious stones for particular months, or for people's birthdays, in Britain until the late nineteenth century. For those with an in-depth knowledge of British folklore, this comes as no surprise. Folklore of the common people is messy, non-systematic and often contradictory. There was, for example, a strong superstition that May was an unlucky month in which to be born, but that does not mean that there was a corresponding belief about all the months. Similarly, Friday was unlucky, and Sunday generally lucky, but there was nothing based on the days of the week until someone wrote the *Monday's Child* rhyme in the mid-nineteenth century. It is the tidying-up behaviour of journalists and popular writers, and those with a commercial interest (i.e., in this case, jewellers), who need to have neat comprehensive schemes.

LUCKY AND UNLUCKY DAYS

Certain days in the year were thought significant, and this followed the general pattern of good or bad reputation attached to those days. It was extremely lucky to be born on Christmas Day, for example, but very bad to arrive on Holy Innocents Day (28 December) which was the day set aside for commemoration of the massacre of the innocents by King Herod, as described in the Bible. An odd belief about Whitsun was recorded a number of times in Ireland but not, it seems, elsewhere in the British Isles:

> On Whit Sunday a child was born to Pat Mitchell, a labourer. It is said that the child born on that day is fated to kill or be killed. To avert this doom a little grave was made, and the infant laid therein, with clay lightly sprinkled on it, and supported by twigs, covering the whole. Thus was the child buried, and at its resurrection deemed to be freed from the malediction.
>
> County Kildare, 1821

As regards the best day of the week on which to make an appearance, there were only a few relevant beliefs, apart from the *Monday's Child* rhyme. It is precisely the fact that this rhyme gives a schematic for the full week that betrays its modern literary origin. In general superstition, Friday was the only day seen as inherently unlucky, and Sunday was generally a lucky one:

As soon as the baby was born, the top of its head was carefully washed with rum, and if it happened that the birth was on a Friday, the child was immediately placed upon a Bible.

Cumberland, 1929

It is lucky to be born on a Sunday; because you can see spirits, and tame the dragon who watches over hidden treasure.

Devon, 1900

A child born on Sunday will be fortunate. If born three hours after sunrise on that day, the child will be able to converse with spirits. Babes born on the last two days of the week are said to marry late in life.

Wales, 1909

LUCKY AND UNLUCKY HOURS

The most widely reported superstition regarding the time of day that a birth took place was undoubtedly that of the 'chime hours', and an infant born at these times was often dubbed a 'chime child'. Unfortunately, there is no general agreement about what exactly constitutes the 'chime hours'. Whereas many claim them to be the hours of three, six, nine and twelve, others were equally certain that four, eight and twelve were the key times. Either way, the belief was that persons born exactly at these times would be supernaturally gifted. They would be able to see fairies and ghosts, would have powers of healing, second sight and so on, and would be generally favoured by fortune all their lives. However the chimes were counted, all were agreed that twelve midnight was by far the most powerful time of day to be born, particularly if it was midnight on one of the special days of the year – notably Christmas Eve, New Year's Eve or Hallowe'en:

> My sister was told by a peasant woman that a 'midnight child' has peculiar gifts: 'it can see everything' – that is spirits and other supernatural beings. My sister has also lately been told that the old nurse of a young man who is a clever amateur actor attributes his powers to the fact that he was born at midnight. It is a common belief that people born on the midnight which links Christmas Eve and Christmas Day have wonderful gifts; but it is new to us that all midnight children are endowed beyond others.
>
> Lincolnshire, 1899

A few other, less widely reported, superstitions claimed a connection between character and the time of day at which the birth takes place. Several made a distinction between babies born at night and babies born during the day, as in the following, recorded in Ireland by Lady Wilde in 1888:

> People born in the morning cannot see spirits or the fairy world; but those born at night have power over ghosts, and can see the spirits of the dead.

Despite the fact that these beliefs have an archaic ring, there is no evidence that they existed before the 1840s, and they may well have been pieces of Victorian Gothic romantic imagination.

TIDES AND PHASES OF THE MOON

It was generally accepted that it was best for babies to be born while the moon was waxing rather than waning, and while the tide was coming in. Many believed that the state of the moon at the time of birth affected a baby's character, or influenced the good or bad luck the baby could expect to enjoy. Thomas Hardy included such a belief in his novel *The Return of the Native* (1878):

> 'Do ye really think it serious, Mister Fairway, that there was no moon?' 'Yes, no moon, no man, 'tis one of the truest sayings ever spit out. The boy never comes to anything that's born at new moon. A bad job for thee that you should have showed your nose then of all days in the month.'

Others went into more detail:

> The Welsh peasantry believe that children born when the moon is new will be very eloquent. Those born at the last quarter will have excellent reasoning powers. Girls born while the moon is waxing will be precocious.
>
> Wales, 1909

Also widespread was the notion that the sex of the next child
born to a family could be predicted through observation of
the phase of the moon at the time of the first child's birth, as
recorded in Cornwall in 1905:

> A popular notion amongst old folks is, that when a boy
> is born on the waning moon the next birth will be a
> girl, and vice versa. They also say that when a birth
> takes place on the growing of the moon, the next child
> would be of the same sex. A child born in the interval
> between the old and the new moons is fated to die
> young.

In coastal areas, the state of the tide was credited with
similar influence and was watched as closely as the moon. It
was generally believed, all across Europe, that in the natural
order of things, babies were born with the incoming tide, and
people died when it was going out. Shakespeare, for
example, in *Henry V*, refers to Falstaff dying with the tide,
and 250 years later, in Charles Dickens's novel *David
Copperfield* (1850), the hero stands beside the deathbed of his
friend Barkis:

> 'He's going out with the tide,' said Mr Peggotty to me,
> behind his hand. My eyes were dim, and so were Mr
> Peggotty's, but I repeated in a whisper, 'With the tide?'
> 'People can't die, along the coast,' said Mr Peggotty,
> 'except when the tide's pretty nigh out. They can't be

born, unless it's pretty nigh in – not properly born, till flood . . . If he lives till it turns, he'll hold his own till past the flood, and go out with the next tide.'

The Moment of Birth

It is not just the time of the birth that can predict the child's future. Their appearance and behaviour directly after the birth was also thought to contain many signs.

BORN WITH A 'CAUL'

One of the most fortunate things that could happen to a person was to be born with a 'caul' – a section of the amniotic membrane draped across the head and face.

> When a child is born with a mask or caul over its head, good luck will follow it all the days of its life, always provided the caul is properly preserved. There is some rite in the preservation of such . . . Some just dried such a covering by laying it between two layers of muslin . . . others wrapped it round the Bible.

This was recorded in Yorkshire in 1898, but the belief was found all over Britain and Ireland, back at least to 1500, and probably much earlier. The most important quality that a caul possessed was that it saved the owner from drowning. Some claimed that a person born with the caul was forever safe from a watery grave, while others believed that the protection only lasted while it was preserved intact. Even more, however, believed that the protection went with mere possession of the item, and that the luck could be transferred to a new owner. Cauls were therefore eagerly sought after by fishermen and sailors, who valued such protection in their daily work. Cauls often changed hands for substantial sums of money, and were frequently advertised in shop windows near the docks, or in newspapers. *The Times* Digital Archive, for example, throws up four occasions between 1793 and 1812 on which cauls were advertised for sale in that paper:

> To persons going to sea – a Caul to be sold; the lowest price is fifteen guineas. Enquire at Mr Wells's, Engraver, No. 137, High Holborn.
>
> 8 April 1793

Apart from its efficacy in preventing drowning, a caul operated on other levels affecting the health and welfare of its owner, and even functioned as an indicator of current well-being and prospects, as recorded by the folklorist William Henderson in northern England in the 1870s:

Within the last five years, in one of our northern cities, a servant was found by her mistress in a state of dejection, for which at first there seemed no assignable cause. After much questioning, the lady elicited that her servant had been born with a veil over her head, which was now presaging evil to her. The veil, she said, had been carefully preserved by her mother, who had entrusted it to her on coming to a woman's estate. It had been stretched and dried, and so had remained over many years. The girl kept it locked in her chest of drawers, and regularly consulted it as her oracle and adviser. If danger threatened her, the veil shrivelled up; if sickness, the veil became damp. When good fortune was at hand the veil laid itself smoothly out; and if people at a distance were telling lies about her, the veil would rustle in its paper. Again, the veil did not like her to cut her hair. If she did so, the veil became uneasy. The owner firmly believed that when she died the veil would disappear. She regarded it with mysterious awe, and only allowed her most intimate friends to know of its existence.

BORN FEET FIRST

It has always been the norm for babies to be born head first, but even today some are born 'breech', i.e. bottom first. Rarer still are babies who are born feet first, so perhaps it is unsurprising that they have given rise to a superstition:

A child born feet first was held to be either possessed of the gift of second sight, or to be born 'a wanderer in foreign countries'.

Fife fishing community, 1912

LOUD CRYING

Long gone are the days when a baby would be held upside down and smacked directly after the birth to induce crying. We are more gentle nowadays, but there is no doubt that wailing and tears after birth are a good sign. From a medical point of view, they show that the child can breathe well and has good reflexes; from the superstitious point of view, loud crying could be interpreted as the sign of a good singer, or, more obscurely, intelligence:

If a child cries lustily after it is born, the bystanders say, 'It's gat a good brain, ony-wye.' 'Ye may say what ye like, but I ken this o't,' said an old woman, 'oot o' a' my ten, my auldest laddie wis the only one that grat [cried] maist awful when he wis born, an' he's been cleverer than ony o' them.'

Aberdeenshire, 1914

THE BABY'S APPEARANCE

There were many aspects of a child's appearance that were thought to hold predictions for the future. A child born with a 'double crown' would live to be a hundred (Norfolk, 1929), or be lucky in money matters (Wales, 1909); a child with small ears would never grow to be rich, while a babe with very large ears would turn out to be selfish and a great talker (Wales, 1909). In Dorset it was considered a lucky omen if a baby girl resembled her father or a baby boy his mother.

THE FIRST THING THE BABY HOLDS

Many parents speak of the moment their child first grabs on to their finger as one of the most moving parts of the birth, and superstitious people of the past also saw great significance in that first clutch. In early twentieth-century Wales it was reported that 'whatever a baby first clutches will indicate its future occupation', and at the same time in the fishing communities around Fife a test had been devised to predict the child's future behaviour:

> If a young child on being given a piece of money, holds it tight, it will turn out to be 'awfu' grippy' (greedy); but if the money slips through its fingers it will be openhanded and generous.

Fife, 1912

Monday's Child

Monday's child is fair of face,
Tuesday's child is full of grace,
Wednesday's child is full of woe,
Thursday's child has far to go,
Friday's child is loving and giving,
Saturday's child works hard for a living,
But the child who is born on the Sabbath Day,
Is bonny and blithe and good and gay.

These words, noted down in Surrey in 2001 from a woman who had learnt them from her mother many years before, represent a standard modern version of a rhyme which most people will know at least in part. This text is very similar to the earliest known version from the 1830s, but others have also been found, with some internal differences based on the same ideas. The following, for example, was noted in 1877.

Born on Monday, fair in the face,
Born on Tuesday, full of God's grace,
Born on Wednesday, sour and sad,
Born on Thursday, merry and glad,
Born on Friday, worthily given,
Born on Saturday, work hard for your living,
Born on Sunday, you will never know want.

Even though the *Monday's Child* rhyme was widely known, it is something of a mystery. It suddenly springs up in the 1830s, bearing all the hallmarks of a recently composed piece. Its language is rather self-conscious, it is suspiciously bright and cheery, but the detail which most sets it apart is that it treats Friday as a good day to be born, whereas almost everywhere else in British superstition, Friday was the one day which was singled out as very unlucky. It is certainly not an example of ancient wisdom, but who wrote it, and where it was first published, remains completely unknown.

There is an alternative version of the meaning of different birthdays, recorded in the extreme north-eastern part of England in the 1890s. Although it is not so widely known as the rhyme, it appears to sum up the underlying tradition more faithfully, if somewhat gloomily:

If a man-child was born on a Sunday, it was believed that he would live without anxiety and be handsome. If born on a Monday he was certain to be killed. Those born on a Tuesday grew up sinful and perverse, while those born on a Wednesday were waspish in temper. A child born on Thursday, however, was sure to be of a peaceful and easy disposition, though averse to women. Friday was supposed to be the most unlucky day of all, being prophesied that a child born on this day would grow up to be silly, crafty, a thief and a coward, and that he would not live longer than mid-age. If born on a Saturday, his deeds would be renowned; he would live to be an alderman, many things would happen to him, and he would live long.

Newborn Babies

Newly born babies should not be laid on their left sides first,
for they will be awkward in shape and clumsy in movement.

Wales, 1909

Influencing Personality

Some superstitions claimed to be able to predict the baby's future character and personality, but there were equally some beliefs which centred on the idea of the infant as a blank canvas on which characteristics could be imposed – either deliberately, or by accident if those in charge of the baby were sufficiently negligent to let it happen.

THE INFLUENCE OF OTHER PEOPLE

Some people insisted that the first person to hold the baby should be a young maiden, because this would instil habits of gentleness and purity into the formative character. On the same lines, many believed that the first person to kiss the new baby would 'temper' it:

A good-tempered person should be selected as the first to kiss the baby, as the good influence will persist through life. A lady told me that her old nurse was much disturbed because the wrong person had kissed and so 'tempered' the baby.

Norfolk, 1929

THE INFLUENCE OF BABY CLOTHES

Care was taken, for example, over what the baby was first wrapped in after birth, as this too could influence future character – 'if a newborn babe is wrapped in fur, its hair will be curly'. 'The baby should be wrapped in an old shirt of its father's, to ensure it being strong' was also recorded in Norfolk in 1929, but in other cases the nurse would be keen to wrap a boy baby in something of the mother's, and a girl in something of the father's. This 'cross-dressing' at birth ensured that the child would be attractive to the opposite sex when grown up, and would therefore have good marriage prospects. The idea seems to have been particularly well known in Scotland. John Macdonald (1741–96), for example, recorded in his *Memoirs of an Eighteenth-Century Footman* that he became so famous in Edinburgh for his success with the ladies that he found it very difficult to find a place and was advised to move to London:

And the servants in Edinburgh said, 'Damn you, Macdonald, I suppose when you was born you was thrown into a woman's shift, and that the women and you are still striving for it.'

'GOING UP IN THE WORLD'

Some superstitions are very obscure and we wonder how on earth they could possibly have developed. Others, however, are based on such transparent symbolism that they seem charmingly simple. So, for example, we all want our children to 'go up in the world', and the most direct way to ensure this is to make the baby's first movement upwards. Stanley Baldwin, born in Worcestershire in 1867, recorded in his memoirs:

> On the day that I was born, our cook, who was a Bewdley woman, wrapped me in a blanket, and to insure that I should rise in life she did the proper thing – she carried me up some stairs. But she wanted my life to be a considerable one, so she tramped up to the top of the house and when she got there she put a chair in the middle of one of the attic rooms, got on it with me in her arms, and then held me up.

The cook's actions obviously worked, as Baldwin became one of the leading politicians of inter-war Britain, serving as prime minister three times, and was created the first Earl of Bewdley in 1937 in recognition of his service to the country.

This was a surprisingly widespread superstition, reported from all parts of England and Scotland from the 1850s onwards, but as most people were born in upstairs bedrooms it sometimes called for creative thinking on the part of the adults involved:

> One good old monthly nurse, in the West Riding, finding there was no higher storey than the one the baby was in, before taking it downstairs for the first time placed a chair on the dressing-table and climbed with the baby to the top of that, exclaiming, 'There, bless its little heart, it shall not go downstairs first.'
>
> Yorkshire, 1878

The earliest definite reference to the belief occurs in the mid-nineteenth century, but it may be much older, as a character in William Congreve's famous Restoration comedy *Love for Love* (1695) claims 'I came upstairs into the world, for I was born in a cellar'.

The Christening

Baptism was one of the first rites to be instituted in the early Christian faith, and all the major Christian sects have some form of baptism through which a newborn baby, or other newcomer, is welcomed and confirmed into the church and the community of the saved. It also formalises the business of the naming of new babies.

HOME CHRISTENING

Babies who were christened at home were sometimes referred to as 'half-baptised', and it was generally expected that the parents would bring the child to church soon after for a public confirmation that the baptism had been properly carried out, as recorded by the eighteenth-century Norfolk cleric Parson Woodforde in his diary:

1 October 1777

Harry Donnell behaved very impertinent this morning
to me because I would not privately name his child for
him, he having one child before named privately by me
and never had it brought to church afterwards. He had
the impudence to tell me he would send it to some
Meeting House to be named etc. – very saucy indeed.

CHRISTENING AS A CURE

Given the importance of the rite of baptism, and the complex
nature of its spiritual meaning, it is hardly surprising that
ordinary folk developed traditions and beliefs of their own,
which existed alongside the official rhetoric. For example,
folk took the idea of the spiritual change wrought by baptism
and added their own, more homely and practical, notions, as
recorded in Derbyshire in 1895:

> Children who are ill-tempered before baptism will be
> good-tempered after they have been baptised. They will
> also sleep better and thrive better. In this respect
> baptism acts as a charm.

Christening could also be more directly medicinal:

> I have heard old people in many places say of sickly
> infants, 'Ah, there will be a change when he has been
> taken to church! Children never thrive until they have

been christened.' Another informs me that about five years ago an instance came under his notice of the healing power supposed to be wrought by baptism as regards the body. The infant child of a chimney-sweeper at Thorne, in the West Riding of Yorkshire, was in a very weak state of health, and appeared to be pining away. A neighbour looked in, and inquired if the child had been baptised. On the answer being given in the negative, she gravely said, 'I would try having it christened.' The counsel was taken, and I believe with success.

Northumberland, 1879

THE POWER OF BAPTISMAL WATER

Even something as obscure as sleepwalking could be cured by the water used in a christening:

A cure for somnambulism was performed by pouring some of the baptismal water on the patient, while awake, but when occupied in conversation or otherwise, in so unexpected a manner as to cause a temporary shock. There are two females in my immediate neighbourhood who have been so treated within the last forty years.

Hebrides, 1900

That this was no recent idea is shown by an extract from *The Image of Idlenesse* (1581):

Among other pleasant talk, he showed her how he
doubted that he was not well christened: for, as he said,
he used oftentimes to rise out of his bed in his sleep, and
going about the house, should do he wist not what
himself.

The water used in the baptismal rite also took on medicinal,
even magical, properties:

 Within the recollection of the present vicar of the parish
of Churcham, Gloucestershire, after public baptism the
then parish monthly nurse invariably washed out the
mouth of the recently regenerated infant with the
remaining sanctified water. She assured the vicar it was
a safeguard against toothache.

Gloucestershire, 1874

It was once prevalent when a child was baptised, that the
infant was neither washed nor bathed that night, for fear
of washing off the baptismal water before it had slept
under it . . . It is reckoned very unlucky in some parts of
the country to have a child left unbaptised beyond the
year in which it was born. For example, should a child
come into the world on the 30 December, 1877, the
parents would feel very uncomfortable, and consider it a
neglect of duty, if they did not get the infant baptised on
that or next day.

Highland Scotland, 1937

In sprinkling the water, all care had to be used to keep it from entering the eyes, as it was believed that the least drop of it entering the eyes opened them to the seeing of ghosts in the journey of life.

Northeast Scotland, 1874

The same writer comments that drinking the water was a way to strengthen the memory.

THE TIME OF THE CHRISTENING

Any aspect of a christening could be subject to superstition, but the timing of the ceremony does not seem to have attracted many beliefs. People liked it to take place on a Sunday, for obvious reasons; some followed the general dislike of Fridays and avoided that day:

Christenings never take place on Fridays in Wales. The old people say, 'The child that is christened on Friday will grow up to be a rogue.'

Wales, 1909

The time of day is rarely mentioned, but follows closely the same ideas noted for time of birth (see p.50)

Children baptised after dark will see 'bokies' [ghosts].

Aberdeenshire, 1914

CRYING AT THE CHRISTENING

In the nineteenth and twentieth centuries, by far the most widespread superstition associated with the christening itself was the idea that it was very unlucky if the baby did not cry during the ceremony, as in this from Devon in 1900:

> It is unlucky for a child to refrain from crying when presented at the font for baptism. It is thought the more it yells and screams, the quicker the evil spirits will quit it.

The supposed penalty for non-compliance in this respect was serious. Although most later reports simply stated that it was 'unlucky', earlier ones were more explicit in their assertion that the infant who did not cry was 'too good for this world', and would not live long. The rationale behind the superstition was that the crying was occasioned by the Devil being forced out by the baptismal rite (a reflection of the notion of 'original sin'):

> In the North, as in the South of England, nurses think it lucky for the child to cry at its baptism; they say that otherwise the baby shows that it is too good to live. Some, however, declare that this cry betokens the pangs of the new birth; some that it is the voice of the evil spirit as he is driven out by the baptismal water.

Nurses and godparents down the ages knew well how to ensure the baby in their charge cried at the given moment:

> When the water fell upon the child, unless it cried it was augured that it would be short-lived, and it is said that, if it did not cry, the woman who received it from the father handled it roughly, or even pinched it, to make it utter the desired cry.
>
> Northeast Scotland, 1874

Such ideas were encountered throughout the British Isles, from at least the 1790s onwards. But it must be said that, very occasionally, the opposite is recorded, and there were also a few completely different interpretations. In Wales, in 1909, it was recorded that 'children that cried at their christening would never live to a great age', and in the Channel Islands, five years later, 'if a baby cries at its baptism it is a sign that it will be cross and peevish all its life'.

MULTIPLE CHRISTENINGS

When more than one child was presented for christening at the same ceremony, the order in which they were christened was dictated by a range of superstitions:

> If there were three babies being christened at the same
> time, the central place was accounted the least favour-
> able, for the middle child to be 'done' would not be
> expected to thrive.

This was in Guernsey, but the most widespread concern was
that boys and girls should be presented in the right order:

> A few years ago [early 1930s], I was baptising two or
> three children at the same time, in a village nearby [in
> Highland Scotland], when the first presented was a boy,
> and the next a girl. After the water had been sprinkled on
> the face of the boy, and when I was about to do the same
> to the girl, an old worthy granny present hastily snatched
> away the bowl containing the water, poured it out, and
> filled it afresh, muttering aloud, 'Goodness forbid that
> my lassie should have a beard.'

If the babies were christened in the wrong order, the girls
would have beards and the boys would have none – a neat
metaphor for wider concerns about relative masculinity and
femininity, or, as one Lancashire woman put it in the 1960s,
'otherwise he will be a namby-pamby and the girl a hoyden'.

There is, in fact, evidence that in the medieval church it
was official policy to christen boys before girls, which is not
surprising given the male bias of all the major religions.
Nevertheless, in the many examples of this superstition
collected in the last two hundred years, a significant minority

had it the other way round and claimed that if the boys were christened first they would 'leave their beards in the water' for the girls to pick up. There were, again, a handful of different interpretations, and many people simply disliked the practice of using the same water to christen more than one baby, whatever the order, and went to great lengths to prevent this from happening, as in the following two examples from Devon (1927 and 1939 respectively):

> If two infants are baptised at the same time, the last which the minister takes will not thrive, but be sickly.

> When one of my children was baptised, my nurse, a very homely woman, took great care to have our baby baptised first, as there was another child to be baptised. I asked her afterwards why she was so anxious about it. Her answer was, 'When the two babies grows up, the first child to be baptised will never serve or be under the second one.' The second child, by the way, is now a Cathedral Canon.

FONTS

A curious belief, recorded in the *Huddersfield Examiner* (26 November 1910), showed that it was thought very unlucky to be the first child baptised in a brand-new font:

A blacksmith there had seven daughters and then a son was born. A few days before the consecration of the new church he came to the vicar, begging him to baptise his boy in the temporary church font. 'Why Joseph, if you will only wait till Thursday the child can be baptised in the new font at the opening of the new church.' 'Thank you, sir,' said the blacksmith with a wriggle, 'but, you see, it's a lad and we should be sorry if he were to dee; na, if 't had been a lass, why, then, you were welcome, for 'twouldn't a' mattered, not a ha'penny. Lasses be ower many, an' lads ower few wi' us.'

The reluctance to use a new font has so far only been found in nineteenth- and early twentieth-century sources, but it may explain something that puzzled church authorities in the Middle Ages. At that time, fonts were re-hallowed with elaborate ceremonies twice a year – at Easter and Whitsun. It was noticed that few babies were presented for baptism at those times, but plenty were always available just before, and a short time afterwards.

CHRISTENING CLOTHES

Almost every detail of a christening could take on symbolic meaning, including even the clothes in which the baby was dressed. Folklorist Walter Gregor, collecting material in northeast Scotland in the 1870s, was told, 'the child must sleep in its baptismal dress', and the same was said on the English side of the border about the same time:

It is the custom in Northumberland to make the chrisom-child sleep the first night in the cap he wore at baptism. 'Loud murmurs,' said my friend, 'arose against me early in my ministerial life for applying so much water that the cap had to be taken off and dried, whereas it should be left on till the next morning. I threw the blame on the modern caps, with their expanse of frilling, on which the good woman said that I was quite right. She has an old christening cap, the heirloom of a friend, which she could show me, of a very different make. Accordingly, I examined the cap, which was evidently very old, and made with reference to affusion in baptism. It excluded forehead, ears and chin, and apparently never had strings. I said that if a mother would bring her baby in such a cap I would undertake not to wet it.

'CHRISTENING PIECES'

One charming custom, which was taken for granted in some areas in the north of England by locals but which took strangers completely by surprise, was the giving of a 'christening piece':

My nephew met a woman carrying a baby in the lane by the church at Humshaugh. Without saying a word to him she put a parcel into his hand and walked off as quickly as she could. The parcel contained a piece of cake and three pennies. My nephew was the only person in the lane at the time. The baby had just been christened, and our cook (an old Northumberland woman) said that they always did this at a christening, but that it ought to have been threepence in silver, not in copper; it had to be given to the first person the christening party saw – man, woman or child.

Northumberland, 1912

Giving such a gift to a passer-by was common in some parts of the country. The gift itself was variously called the 'christening piece', 'bairn's piece', 'christening crib' or 'kimbly', or was known by some other local name. The gift always contained something to eat and some money, and occasionally other items as well. In most cases it was simply given to the first person met, but in others the choice of recipient was more complex:

A cottager whose ancestors had lived for generations on Dartmoor had four children, all girls. At each christening she had baked a small saffron cake, and on the way to church, the first male they met, she gave him the cake neatly wrapped in paper for luck; if the baby had been a boy, the cake would be given to the first female they met.

Devon, 1906

The luck of the baby depended on the recipient taking the piece and doing the right things in return. Donors took the matter very seriously, and could be quite insistent, as in this example from western Scotland in 1879:

It was of importance that the person who received this gift should be lucky – should have lucky marks upon their person. Forecasts were made from such facts as the following concerning the recipient of the gift – Was this person male or female, deformed, disfigured, plain-soled, etc.? If the party accepted the gift willingly, tasted it, and returned a few steps with the baptismal party, this was a good sign; if they asked to look at the baby, and blessed it, this was still more favourable. But should this person refuse the gift, nor taste it, nor turn back, this was tantamount to wishing evil to the child, and should any serious calamity befall the child, even years after, it was connected with this circumstance, and the party who had refused the baptismal gift was blamed for the evil which had befallen the child.

The first concrete reference to this practice is from Glasgow in the 1820s, but it was clearly already an established custom at that time, It was still going strong in that area in the 1950s. It does not seem to have been found all over the British Isles, being widespread in Scotland, northern England and the Isle of Man, and also known in the West Country and in Wales, but being apparently unknown in other parts of England. In areas where the custom took place, it was not unusual for children to hang around church gates at weekends in case a christening party came out, in the hope of getting the 'piece' for themselves.

TRADITIONAL GIFTS

The tradition of giving a new baby symbolic gifts when you first meet it was very widely practised across Britain, from the late eighteenth century onwards, and probably before that time as well. The vital importance of beginnings is a fundamental principle of superstition, and it is no surprise to find it reflected in this context:

> The custom of giving to a baby, on its first visit to a friend's house, bread, salt and egg, and a silver coin, with occasionally a packet of sugar, is still observed in the West Riding of Yorkshire and in the county of Durham. My children usually returned from their first excursion with quite a load of these provisions.
>
> 1878

In some areas this was called 'handselling' the baby, which means bringing luck with a first gift or sale. Money was always included, and eggs, bread and salt were the most widely reported gifts, although others, such as matches and even shoes, were local variations on the theme. The money could be used as a test of the baby's future financial acuity, and there were other little traditions involved, as recorded in Cumberland in 1929, though here the visit is being made *to* the baby's home:

Another custom was to take a new-laid hen's egg, a small packet of salt, and a sixpence when paying a first visit to a newly-made mother. The coin was placed in the infant's right hand; if it is grasped and held it was a sign of tightfistedness; if held loosely, of generosity; if it fell to the ground, of prodigality. The first egg received was generally blown and kept, the donor's name being written on it, but other eggs were used as usual.

Some used the eggs and other foodstuffs as ingredients for the christening cake, which may explain why the custom was called 'puddening' the baby in some parts of Yorkshire. By the second half of the twentieth century, the custom was in decline and if it continues anywhere today it would be a rare survival. The tradition of giving a coin to the baby has lasted longest, and a few people still feel the need to do this.

Godparents

Godparents (also called sponsors or witnesses) were formerly very important figures in the life of a child in Britain, and for some families still are. At the christening, they undertake to ensure that the child receives a proper Christian upbringing. They speak on behalf of the child and make promises to renounce the Devil and obey the teachings of the Church. A wide range of beliefs and customs became associated with the role of godparents over the years.

SELECTING GODPARENTS

As with all the other adult principals involved in a christening ceremony, even small details of the godparents' behaviour could seriously affect the child's future. In Wales, in 1909, for example:

People formerly said if you wanted your children to attain a long age, you should see that the godparents come from three different parishes . . . If a sponsor looked around during the christening ceremony, the child would be able to see ghosts . . . If the godparents refused any dish at the christening feast, the babe would dislike that food all through life. If the sponsors whispered during a christening, the babe would walk and talk in its sleep.

Similar beliefs were recorded in Staffordshire in the 1880s, claiming that if godparents looked into the font during the christening, the child would grow up to resemble them.

Superstition also placed restrictions on those eligible to stand as godparents. Potential godparents needed to take note of their own situation:

A married woman living at Eardisland refused to be a godmother to her sister's child, because she had been told that if she did so, she would have no children herself.

Herefordshire, 1912

And in Devon a decade earlier:

It is unlucky for an unmarried person to be sponsor at a baptism; for, 'First to the font, never to the altar.'

But it could also be perilous for the baby:

> If a sponsor stands for two children in one year, it is
> believed that one of them will die. Sometimes the
> sponsors ask some request of God for the child and their
> request is certainly granted.
>
> Wexford, 1936

Perhaps the last comment and the request makes up for all the
other strictures and dangers.

'GOD-CAKES'

A charming custom was recalled by Elizabeth Mary Wright,
an expert on folklore and dialect born in 1863:

> An ancient custom in the city of Coventry is the sending
> of 'god-cakes' on New Year's Day. The god-cake is a
> particular kind of cake sent by godparents to their
> godchildren. It varies in price, but its shape is invariably
> triangular, it is about one inch thick, and is filled with
> mincemeat. A similar custom exists in Kidderminster,
> where the head of the family sends out packets of
> 'blessing-cakes' to the scattered representatives of the
> original stock, wherever they may be. Each householder
> who receives a gift of cakes must again distribute them
> among the members of the household, servants included,
> so that every one under his roof may receive a family

blessing. The cakes are long oval buns, rather thin, coated on the top with melted sugar, and ornamented with seven sultanas. As my father came from Kidderminster, I have eaten blessing-cakes every New Year's Day as far back as my memory carries me, but I was never clear as to the significance of the seven sultanas. I think they are intended to symbolise a sevenfold blessing.

Choosing a Name

Choosing a name for a baby is rarely a simple process, even today, but we should spare a thought for our ancestors, who had to consider numerous factors that are now ignored. Many previously held convictions have disappeared simply because of changing fashions, while others have fallen victim to feelings of increasing independence on the part of parents and the loosening of control exerted by family members, religious leaders and other officials.

There are many tales of vicars in the past refusing to baptise a baby with a particular name, or of officious local registrars who would not issue certificates for a Bobby or Maggie, but insisted on Robert or Margaret for official purposes. Sometimes this officiousness was helpful, as in the case of a mother who asked for her baby to be christened Cain because she thought that he was the 'good' one in the Cain and Abel story in the Bible. But errors of this kind are not entirely a thing of the past. According to the *Daily Sport* (11 November 1993), the vicar of St Andrew's, Litherland, Merseyside, refused outright to christen a child Damien because that name had acquired such a bad reputation from the horror film trilogy *The Omen*, in which Satan returned to earth as a baby so-named. The mother had reportedly chosen the name because her son was 'a little devil'. People called Damien should not despair, however, as the name has been known in England since at least the thirteenth century, and there was a St Damian centuries before Hollywood rebranded the name.

At the root of such prejudices is the ancient notion that, as recorded in Highland Scotland in 1926, 'the child is supposed to take the character after whom it is named'. This idea of 'naming after' also extends to the animal kingdom:

It is unlucky to bestow the name of any animal; a farmer near Cusop called his little girl Chloe, after his favourite mare. Believers in this superstition were of course confirmed in their faith when, at the age of three, the child was burnt to death in the rickyard, and the mare fell and broke her back shortly afterwards at the same spot. On the other hand, it is lucky for the child if the initials of its full name spell a word, and the baptismal name or names are sometimes chosen with regard to this point.

Herefordshire, 1912

This belief about initials is only rarely reported, and has never been explained.

REUSING NAMES

Nowadays, we would not even think of giving the same name to another baby if a child dies, but this practice was not at all uncommon in the past. A discussion published in the journal *Notes & Queries* in 1888, for example, noted that Edward III had three sons called William, and subsequent correspondents confirmed that the practice was not confined to royalty but was quite commonly found in villages around the country. Some, however, thought it very unlucky to reuse a name in this way: 'It is strange, but in my knowledge of families I have never known a child survive who was called after another previously dead,' commented one contributor, although others cited many instances in their experience where this was not the case. In the same journal, in 1910, a correspondent noted:

> In Ireland it is regarded as a certain way of bringing ill-luck and early death to 'call a child for' a dead brother or sister [because] the name is already registered in Heaven.

FAMILY NAMES

Then there is the question of babies being 'named after' other people – grandparents, uncles, aunts, friends of the family, and so on. If you please one, you upset the others, and anyway Grandad's name, which was perfectly acceptable sixty years ago, may not be so now.

It will come as no surprise to modern readers to learn that the pressure to name a child after a particular person was much stronger in the past. Go back a few generations and many families can boast a whole string of fathers and sons or mothers and daughters all bearing the same first name. Favourite uncles and aunts were another source of names, and it was even considered a pleasing compliment for the baby to be named after the clergyman who was conducting the baptism, especially if it was his first time carrying out the ceremony. It was fortunate that in large families there were several opportunities to keep everyone satisfied.

One of the strongest traditions was to name the baby after the principal godparent. This has a long history: figures quoted by Barbara Hanawalt in her study of peasant families in fifteenth-century England, for example, reveal that 65–87 per cent of people at that time had the same first name as their godparents. On the other hand, this may not have been totally from choice, as there was a severely restricted pool of names from which to choose. In the late thirteenth century, in three whole villages, there were only 36 different male names and 20 female names, while in tenant lists for fourteenth- and fifteenth-century manors only 11 male names and 10 for females appeared.

SAINTS' NAMES

Saints' names were popular in many families, especially if the baby was born on a particular saint's feast day. Parson Woodforde, the eighteenth-century diarist, wrote:

> 27 March 1765
> I christened two children (twins) of Robin Francis's this afternoon . . . by the names of Joseph and Mary, being born on Lady Day last.

On the other hand, some believed that it was unlucky to choose a saint's name, because 'the saints would want it' and the baby would soon die. Biblical names in general were very popular until the late nineteenth century, as this story recorded amongst the colliers of Staffordshire shows:

> Sometimes the Bible is opened, and the first name that occurs is chosen. My informant knew four brothers, respectable young men, called Matthew, Mark, Luke and John. It is said that three little boys, new comers, presented themselves one Sunday morning at the Dawley schools, and gave their names as Daniel, Shadrach and Meshach. 'Daniel, Shadrach, and Meshach!' said the

amused parson to whom they spoke, 'and where's Abednego?' 'Please sir, he's a-bed i' the cradle,' was the unexpected reply.

STICKING TO A NAME

On top of all the concerns about which name to choose, there were also superstitions that suggested it was extremely bad luck to change your mind:

> Before the baby is nine days old it is wise to decide upon its name, and once having done this, *so let it be*. If either parent should happen to say, 'We will call it so-and-so', do not alter after having so declared, for if so the child will grow up a liar, and probably have to assume several aliases before death. But the worst of all is to decide upon a name before the child is born, and then afterwards change to some other.

> Yorkshire, 1898

KEEPING NAMES SECRET

Probably the most widespread and deep-rooted concern in past times was to keep the baby's name a secret until it was christened:

The name of the baby is decided by the father, and is never told to anyone outside the family. I have often asked, 'What is baby's name to be?' and, if the parents are really country folk, the reply is always evasive, 'We don't know yet', or 'We haven't thought about it.'

Herefordshire, 1912

There is first the danger of the stupid women, and stupider men, who will persist in asking what the child's name is, though all ought to know that it is very unlucky to divulge it until it is first pronounced by the officiating clergyman. And strange are the dodges to ensure this, the most common still being the handing of a slip of paper with the baby's name on it to the minister when he asks the father what the child's name is.

Highland Scotland, 1926

And, similarly:

A baby's name should not be made public until after the christening, otherwise *les p'tites gens* [the fairies] might become aware of his existence and exchange him for one of their own bantlings whilst he was still in an unbaptised state. As nobody believes in fairies any more, names of newborn infants are now usually announced with the birth notice in the local paper.

Guernsey, 1975

In this last example, the reason behind the reluctance to announce the baby's name prematurely is explicitly to protect the child from evil-wishers, but a more common notion at play here was the fear of 'tempting fate' – announcing the name before the child has officially reached the naming stage is seen as pride, and parents will be punished for their arrogance. A third possibility may even be an excess of religious sensitivity – the naming of the child is in God's hands, and should not be pre-empted.

There were many other name superstitions which could be cited, but none so strange, perhaps, as the bald statement included in a list of 'North Lincolnshire Folk-Lore' published in *Notes & Queries* in 1853: 'Persons called Agnes always go mad.' It is to be hoped that this superstition, at least, is incorrect.

Churching

In previous times, the first thing most mothers would do after recovering from giving birth would be to visit their church for a ceremony by which they were welcomed back into the Christian community, just as their baby had been welcomed into it by christening, a few days before. There has always been a tension in the Western Church over how the ceremony of churching should be viewed. The references in the Bible, based on much older Jewish traditions, are definitely couched in terms of the necessary purification of the mother after a birth, but there has long been a move towards regarding it as an opportunity for thanksgiving

RESTRICTIONS ON THE NEW MOTHER

It is hardly surprising that a number of superstitions and unofficial beliefs grew up around the occasion of churching, and despite the official attempts to rebrand the rite, these traditional superstitions were unequivocally couched in terms of purification, and were heavily weighted towards constraining the activities of women to a degree that few would even comprehend today. The idea that the first place visited should be the church, for example, led to major restrictions on the movements and activities of new mothers. They were expected to stay at home, quite literally, until they had the opportunity to be churched, and if they did venture out, few in the community would even allow them in their houses:

The mother was under great restrictions till churched. She was not allowed to do any kind of work, at least any kind of work more than the most simple and necessary. Neither was she permitted to enter a neighbour's house, and had she attempted to do so, some would have gone the length of offering a stout resistance, and for the reason that, if there chanced to be in the house a woman great with child, travail would prove difficult with her.

Northeast Scotland, 1874

After the birth of a child the mother will not go down the street or anywhere, even to buy provisions, until she has been churched. This custom causes trouble to the clergy, who are often asked to church women at all sorts of hours so that they may be able to visit their friends or do some shopping.

Cambridgeshire, 1914

> A woman who has given birth to a child may not touch or prepare food which is to be eaten by other members of the family, nor may she touch utensils which they use until she has been to church.
>
> England, 1927

All over the British Isles they were routinely described as 'unlucky', 'uncanny', 'unclean', and so on. There are stories of Irish mothers who would put a piece of their house-thatch in their hats so that they could claim to be still 'under their own roof' while out shopping. Even if this tale is untrue, we have to admire the spirit of independence that it represents.

GETTING TO CHURCH

Notions of impurity and modesty even circumscribed a woman's behaviour on the way to the church for the ceremony, sometimes in surprising ways. She must not look at the sky or even cross the road, and this latter restriction led to the astonishing idea, held not by a few cranks but by many in the population, that the unchurched woman was not even protected by ordinary laws of the land:

> My grandmother used to say, that if a woman after childbirth crossed a cart or wheel rut before she was churched, a man might shoot her, and he could not be punished for it.
>
> Somerset, 1873

The fact that the mother herself is regarded as dangerous confirms that the underlying notions are of pollution and the need for cleansing, but occasionally the traditional beliefs implied that the mothers were also at risk. In the same way that unbaptised babies were considered in danger of being carried away by the fairies, some thought that the mother could also be abducted by the 'good folk', where they were sometimes needed to nurse the fairies' own babies.

This Little Piggie Went to Market

This little piggie went to market,
This little piggie stayed at home,
This little piggie had roast beef,
This little piggie had none,
And this little piggie went wee wee wee
All the way home.

This popular nursery rhyme dates from at least the 1720s, and has been the most common of the finger and toe rhymes for a long time. Many versions of this rhyme have been recorded, but it is unlikely that anyone will want to go back to a version from Shropshire in the 1880s:

This little pig said, I like red wheat,
This little pig said, where do you get it from?
This little pig said, out of Daddy's barn,
This little pig said, I'll tell!
This little pig cried wee, wee, wee! I can't get over the barn-door sill!

Babycare

The wife of a big farmer, converted the labourers' wives on the
farm to greater cleanliness, by taking one pig out of a litter and
washing it well twice daily. The piglet thrived out of all proportion
to its brothers and sisters. The women then said: 'If 'ter good for
pig, 'ter good for were children.'

Norfolk, 1929

Good Parenting

Babies in the first weeks and months of life are both precious and highly vulnerable, and it is hardly surprising that the business of looking after them should have become so hedged about with superstition over the centuries. New parents have always had a vast body of folkloric advice to draw upon, encompassing everything from what to feed their child to how to dress it and when to cut its fingernails.

TEMPTING FATE

For the superstitious person, one of the worst things you can do in life is to 'tempt fate'. Most of us struggle to provide an actual definition of the word 'fate', but we have a deep-rooted feeling that if we are too sure of ourselves, too confident in our future, or too boastful, then something will conspire to trip us up and teach us a lesson. This may simply manifest itself in the idea that if we refuse to take an umbrella, it is sure to rain, but the principle also functions at a much deeper and more serious level, and is so woven into the social fabric of our daily life that we do not really notice it. 'Don't count your chickens' is one of our most oft-quoted proverbs, and there are plenty more, like 'Pride goes before a fall' and 'There's many a slip', to remind us that nothing in life is certain.

The surest sign that someone is aware that they have courted disaster in this respect is when you hear them say 'touch wood', which many of us do instinctively, half jokingly, suiting the action to the words. Incidentally, 'touching wood' has nothing to do with ancient tree spirits, or even the Christian cross, but probably originated with a children's chasing game called 'tiggy tiggy touch wood' around the turn of the nineteenth century. A much older way of covering yourself in such situations was to say 'God willing' or 'God save us', or some other pious protective phrase.

As regards babies, there are numerous examples of the fear of tempting fate, and new parents and parents-to-be may carefully avoid any actions or decisions that could be taken as overconfidence about the future. Many parents still show reluctance to choose a name, or at least to tell it to others, before the baby is born (see p.96), and others are careful not to give gifts too early in the pregnancy. One of the best-known baby superstitions of the twentieth century was that first-time mums-to-be would buy a new pram but make sure that it did not enter the house until after the baby was born, and this idea is far from extinct (see p.147). Even after the baby is born, the 'fate' principle still operates:

> If a mother gives away all the baby's clothes she has (or the cradle), she will be sure to have another baby, though she may have thought herself above such vanities.
>
> Suffolk, 1864

But fate is unpredictable and does not always operate in quite the way we expect. There was a widespread notion, for example, that it was very unlucky to rock an empty cradle. Knowing the ways of superstition, we would expect the result of such action to be that the usual occupant of the cradle would die, but this is not what fate had in store, because rocking the cradle tempts providence to fill it again, with another new baby.

However seriously some superstitious people took these ideas, these examples are relatively trivial, in that they are concerned with isolated incidents and good or bad luck, but in many communities the 'fate' principle so pervaded people's daily lives that it made a real difference to their outlook and the way they lived their lives. Indeed, in many traditional communities it was almost as if it was deemed socially unacceptable to be at all happy, confident or proud. One of the worst social faux pas that a person could commit was to praise a baby: 'Children should not be unduly praised for this is speaking too soon and evil may follow' was how it was expressed in a book of Guernsey folklore published in 1975. The only way to avoid this evil was to say the customary protective formula, as, for example, in the Irish changeling story recounted on p.167, where it was the failure to say 'God bless it!' which put the baby at risk from the fairies.

Notions of tempting fate were often a feature of a deeply pessimistic view of life. Typical was the belief, recorded in Lancashire in 1873, that clever children rarely live long:

> Precocious children are seldom long-lived; they are often reminded that they 'are too fause [wise] to live'.

This particular idea was already proverbial in the sixteenth century, and is casually mentioned by many authors, including Shakespeare in *Richard III* (1591) – 'So wise, so young, they say do never live long' – and Jonathan Swift in *Polite Conversation* (1738) – 'I fear Lady Answerall can't live long, she has so much wit.' Odd as it may seem today, this example of the dread of tempting fate lasted well into the twentieth century:

> 'If a baby a few weeks old takes a lot of notice he won't live to see his twenty-first birthday.
>
> Somerset, 1923

'FORESPEAKING'

Such deep-seated worries were expressed all over the British Isles in one form or another, but some of the reports from northeast and western Scotland reveal a particularly dark view of life. People there had the notion of 'forespeaking', or causing harm by excessive interest or praise:

> It was not deemed proper to bestow a very great deal of praise on a child; and one doing so would have been interrupted by some such words as 'Gueed sake, haud yir tung, or ye'll forespyke the bairn.' Such a notion of forespeaking by bestowing excessive praise was not limited to infants, but extended to full-grown people, to domestic animals, and to crops . . . To guard the child from being 'forespoken', it was passed three times through the petticoat or chemise the mother wore at the time of the accouchement.

The matter was further complicated when superstition and religion combined forces:

> There was also the superadded danger of the mother setting her affections too much upon her child and forgetting God, who then in jealousy and mercy would remove it from her. This latter was a very widespread superstition among religiously-minded people, even among those who, from their education, ought to have

known better. I well remember the case of a young mother – a tender loving woman, who, quite in keeping with her excitable affectionate nature, was passionately fond of her baby, her first-born. But baby sickened and died, and the poor mother, borne down with grief, wept bitterly, like Rachel refusing to be comforted. In the depth of her affliction she was visited by both her pastor and elder. They admonished her to turn her mind from the selfish sorrow in which she was indulging, and thank God for his kindly dealing toward her, in that he had removed from her the cause of sin on her part.

This was reported from western Scotland in 1879. Presumably the people involved thought they were helping, but few today would think it appropriate to confront a bereaved young mother with such narrow-minded and cruel notions.

Daily Routine

An astonishing number of mundane everyday procedures were previously fraught with symbolic meaning and were governed by superstition and traditional belief. These encompassed virtually all the essential tasks performed as a matter of course by new parents, from washing the infant to weighing it, feeding it and otherwise assuming responsibility for its welfare.

WASHING

Washing a newborn baby would seem to be a pretty innocuous procedure, but not so in this Scottish doctor's account:

Having made the baby secure and ready to be bathed, I wrapped it up and handed it over to the women, while I attended to the mother. The mother was in good shape: all was well. I could leave her now and go home. But I must have a look at the baby. There it was lying just as I had left it – unwashed – and four or five women sitting round the fire talking. 'Haven't you washed the baby yet?' said I looking at the woman who had appeared to be in attendance. 'Me! Wash a newborn baby! Na, na, I've never washed a newborn bairn. The doctor has to dae that – or else the nurse.' 'Which of you will wash the baby?' said I looking round. 'Nane o's! Nane o's! I cudna wash a new bairn – it's no lucky. You'll hae to dae it, doctor!'

Dundee, 1960s

It is not known how widespread this particular notion was, but Theo Brown, a folklorist from Devon, commented:

When I was a child, living in the parish of Kingskerswell (Devonshire), my father always stated that children born in the village were never bathed on any account until they were five years old. They were not considered strong enough to bear the experience.

Even where there was no general prohibition on washing, there were various unofficial local rules covering the baby's first wash, and a wide range of substances was used, including different oils, fats, salted water and, quite often, alcohol:

The baby used to be rubbed over with pork lard before it was washed, and bound round with a linen rag, previously thoroughly scorched at the fire till brown. A little gin and water was put on top of its head. The face and hands of the mother were washed with gin and water, 'to remove the tan on face and hands which comes when a woman is carrying a child'.

Suffolk, 1924

Particular attention was given to the baby's head in this respect. In Fife in 1912 it was whisky:

A mouthful of whisky was taken, and skilfully blown as a spray over the child's head, and then massaged in, 'to strengthen the heid'.

But in Cumberland in 1929 it was rum:

As soon as the baby was born, the top of its head was carefully washed with rum.

One of the most widespread superstitions concerning washing babies was the curious idea that it was very unlucky to wash an infant's right hand until it was a year old, or even longer. To do so would prevent the child accumulating wealth in later years:

In washing the newborn infant great care was used not to
let the water touch the palms of the hands, and this care
was continued for a considerable length of time, under
the belief that to wash the palms of the hands washed
away the luck of this world's goods.

Northeast Scotland, 1874

Some mothers compromised by cleaning the worst dirt off
with a damp cloth, but many simply left the hand untouched,
which must have made thumb-sucking a distinctly unhy-
gienic operation. This belief was recorded all across England,
and in Scotland, from mid-Victorian times onwards, and
chimes well with other beliefs from the period concerning
hands. In the wider world of superstition, hands are often
symbolically connected with riches; an itchy right hand, for
example, means money coming in (an itchy left one means
money going out), and as mentioned above, a baby's future
financial acumen could be judged by whether it grasped
tightly the first coin given to it, or let it fall to the ground.

But hands are also the tools of trade of the thief, and there
was sometimes a worry in new parents' minds that their little
darling would take the wrong path through life:

On examining an infant's hand, the mother excused the
dirt of its palm by saying, 'You know we never wash the
palm of an infant's hand: my other child was eighteen
months old before I ever washed his palm.' On
expressing my surprise at such a dirty excuse, she

replied, 'They say, if an infant's palm is washed, it will make it light-fingered.'

County Durham, 1867

WEIGHING

Our modern system of monitoring the health and welfare of new babies relies so heavily on the careful recording of size and weight, that it comes as a real surprise that up to only fifty years ago there were people who were distinctly uneasy about the whole idea of measurement, and many who refused to have their babies weighed at all. The idea was particularly resented when it was just becoming fashionable, as here in Suffolk in 1864:

> It is unlucky to weigh newborn children. If you do, they will probably die, and, at any rate, will not thrive. I have caused great concern in the mind of a worthy old monthly nurse by insisting on weighing mine. They have, however, all done very well, with the exception of one, the weighing of whom was accidentally forgotten to be performed.

These ideas were widely held right up to the Second World War, and it was only the introduction of the National Health Service that finally put paid to them.

It is not entirely clear why there was such a prejudice against weighing and measuring, although the most likely reason is that it was based on the fear of tempting fate. A range of other superstitions had similar notions at their heart. Some people, for example, hated to be precise about numbers in any group, such as a school class, as to do so was to tempt fate to reduce them; farmers' wives disliked counting their chickens; and deep-sea fishermen refused to count their catch, because the next haul would therefore be less, and so on.

FEEDING

In many places there were strong local traditions that dictated what should be given to a baby as their first food immediately after birth. Although the custom was often described in terms of the item being good for the baby, it is clear that the real underlying reason was symbolic rather than dietary, and was therefore a piece of superstition rather than medical science. Fortunately, the babies were not expected to 'eat' the food as such, but a tiny portion was placed in their mouths for them to taste. The most widely reported recipe, across the British Isles, was butter and honey, or sugar:

> As soon as possible after birth a little butter or honey, or, in later days, butter and moist sugar, were placed in the baby's mouth, not merely for sweetness, or even to 'clear its throat', but because honey had many rare virtues attributed to it, whence its name 'Treacle of Heaven'.

This was in Warwickshire in 1930, and the idea was clearly based on a passage in the Old Testament, Isaiah 7:14–15:

Behold, a virgin shall conceive, and bear a son, and shall call his name Immanuel. Butter and honey shall he eat, that he may know to refuse the evil, and choose the good.

Other local variations existed. In Cumberland and Westmorland, for example, a very strong tradition at the gatherings to celebrate the arrival or christening of a new baby was the provision of rum and butter for everybody present, and a tiny portion was placed in the baby's mouth for luck. In other places a red-hot poker, or a cinder from the fire, was placed in water, a little of which, when cooled, was put in the baby's mouth. This was believed to be strengthening and, when the child was a little older, a sure-fire cure for wind.

Some newborns seem to be constantly licking their lips, and this was often taken to be connected with the mother's antenatal 'cravings'.

If the newborn infant seemed restless and made a sucking movement with its lips, it was supposed to show a desire for something its mother had not been able to supply. In Warwickshire this something took the form of hare's brains reduced to a jelly. It was an ordinary custom on the Alscot estate to send a deputation to the lady of the manor to beg a hare's head for the purpose; this custom was kept up to the last thirty years.

1930

'Hare's brains' are often cited in nineteenth-century sources as the epitome of healthy food for invalids, which is strange because the hare hardly has any desirable attributes in itself, and, indeed, hare's meat was normally distrusted and avoided by country folk. Few rural working families would touch it at all under normal circumstances. (See p.26 for further discussion of beliefs concerned with expectant mothers' cravings.)

Another widespread custom in this context involved placing a little salt in the baby's mouth. This was often explained as protecting the child by helping to keep witches at bay, and is therefore presumed to be of pagan origin, but it is again almost certainly based on the Bible, which includes numerous references to salt, including the following, from Ezekiel 16:4, which was probably the direct precursor of the custom in the British Isles:

And as for thy nativity, in the day thou wast born thy navel was not cut, neither wast thou washed in water to supple thee; thou wast not salted at all, nor swaddled at all.

Nursing mothers, meanwhile, were recommended to take lettuce, borage, fennel, aniseed, mint and chamomile, although a passage from Jane Sharp's *The Compleat Midwife's Companion* (1724) shows that 'sympathetic magic' was often as important an ingredient as the herbs:

Some say that by sympathy a cow's udder dried in the oven, first cut into pieces, and then powdered, half a pound of this powder to an ounce of sweet fennel-seed, with two ounces of cummin-seed, and four ounces of sugar, will make milk increase exceedingly.

CUTTING FINGERNAILS

A surprising number of superstitions were concerned with how and when people should cut their fingernails, and these applied equally to small children. It was widely believed, for example, that to do so on a Friday or Sunday was to invite certain misfortune. As Thomas Middleton has one of his characters complain in his play *Any Thing for a Quiet Life* (1621):

What a curst wretch was I to pare my nails today, and a Friday too; I lookt for some mischief.

There was also a rhyme about the other days of the week:

Cut them on Monday, cut them for health,
Cut them on Tuesday, cut them for wealth,
Cut them on Wednesday, cut them for news,
Cut them on Thursday, a pair of new shoes,
Cut them on Friday, cut them for sorrow,
Cut them on Saturday, a present tomorrow,
But he that on Sunday cuts his horn,
Better that he had never been born.

Apart from the prohibition on Friday and Sunday, it is not clear whether this rhyme embodies earlier thinking, as it cannot be found any earlier than 1830. But it was certainly in general circulation from that time until quite recently.

A superstition that applies specifically to babies is that their nails must not be cut during the first year of their life. They can be bitten off by a parent, but must not be cut in the normal way, because if they are, the child will undoubtedly grow up to be 'light-fingered' or a thief. This notion was formerly extremely widespread, being well known from the Channel Islands to the Orkneys. Remarkably, it was still being taken seriously within living memory, as a piece in the journal *Folk-Lore*, in 1960, demonstrates:

> In a letter to the *Sunday Dispatch* of August 7, 1960, a mother at Bridlington, Yorkshire, writes that two mothers have told her quite seriously that to cut her baby's nails before she is a year old would bring bad luck. The way, they say, is to nip them with the teeth. She asks if there could possibly be any medical reason for following this practice? In reply, the Editor says 'No', and gives the old superstition that the baby would grow up to be a thief, and, in Germany, it would grow up with a stammer.

CUTTING HAIR

It is a commonplace of superstition that personal 'effects' such as hair and nails should not be discarded lightly. It was well known that something closely connected with the intended victim is an essential element of any malicious spell, and these removable pieces of the body should therefore be carefully destroyed and not allowed to fall into others' hands:

> It was not necessary that the person possessed of the evil eye, and desirous of inflicting evil upon a child, should see the child. All that was necessary was that the person with the evil eye should get possession of something which had belonged to the child, such as a fragment of clothing, a toy, hair or nail pairings ... I have seen the door locked during hair-cutting, and the floor swept afterwards, and the sweepings burned, lest perchance any hairs remain, and be picked up by an enemy.

This was written in western Scotland in 1879. At about the same time Lady Wilde in Ireland also noted that such items as had an intimate connection with their owners could be used in cures as well as curses:

> Clippings of the hair and nails of a child tied up in a linen cloth and placed under the cradle will cure convulsions.

One last word on the disposal of human hair – another reason for burning or burying cut hair was that wild birds might use carelessly discarded hair to make their nests, and this would cause the owner to suffer severe headaches.

MIRRORS

Adults routinely use mirrors to check their appearance, but it was formerly thought unwise to show a baby its reflection in a mirror:

> A child under one year should not be shown its reflection
> in a mirror for that may stop it growing.
>
> Guernsey, 1975

This was a surprisingly widespread superstition from at least the 1850s until the second half of the twentieth century, although it seems to be completely forgotten nowadays. The predicted effect of doing so varied considerably. Many simply claimed it was 'unlucky', but others claimed it could cause a range of problems, from having trouble with teething to contracting rickets. The only predictions which would seem to have anything approaching a logical basis were that it would make the baby cross-eyed, or, as recorded in Wales in 1909:

> A child who has not yet talked should never be held up
> to a mirror, for this encourages vanity.

In the past, mirrors had a decidedly uncanny reputation and were regarded with deep-seated suspicion by many people. From the Middle Ages, and probably long before, mirrors were used to predict the future and to see things happening a long way off, like a crystal ball. In later periods, it was strongly advised that all mirrors in a house be covered on the death of an occupant, in case the mourners saw a reflection of the deceased in them, and they were also covered up during thunderstorms. At midnight on Hallowe'en, or on other key nights, a girl could stand in front of a mirror, brushing her hair, in the hope of seeing her future husband's reflection looking over her shoulder. Unfortunately, she might see the Devil there instead.

One of the most widely kept superstitions of the present day is that it is very unlucky to break a mirror. This is probably based on the idea that as a mirror reflects the face of a person, anything which happens to it also affects its owner. It may therefore be that by allowing the mirror to reflect the baby's face, power over the child's fate is given to any malevolent person, or simply to fate, to harm the baby by harming the mirror. This interpretation is certainly supported by the linking of mirrors and photographs in the following example from Devon in the early twentieth century:

Until it is a year old a baby should never see itself in a mirror, or be photographed; our nursemaids used to carefully avoid any possibility of the former, and I remember their extreme consternation when one of the

Baby Clothes

No part of human existence escaped the attention of the superstitious, and clothes were no exception. Various superstitions on the subject were equally applicable to both adults and children, the only real difference being that as the baby cannot dress itself the parents have to take the blame (although the baby gets the good or bad luck). Since at least the seventeenth century, for example, a widespread superstition has advised that to put on an item of clothing back-to-front or inside out is a very lucky omen – as long as it is done accidentally. The luck is broken, however, if the error is corrected during the day:

A retired schoolmistress reports that a child in her class arrived at school one morning very distressed as she had fallen and broken her wrist. 'I put my pinafore on inside out, and changed it back,' she said, 'I didn't ought to have done it, did I?'

Dorset

The same rule applied to babies, although in one report, from Wales in 1909, it was suggested as a deliberate policy:

The first time the child is carried out, one of its garments should be put on with the wrong side uppermost for luck.

Another superstition common to adults and children advised that it is lucky to find a thread or pin accidentally left in a new garment. According to Ruth Tongue's collection of Somerset beliefs, published in 1965, this should be done deliberately in a baby's case:

Always leave a pin in a baby's frock until it is christened.

A third general superstition that applied equally to adults and children held that it is very unlucky to mend clothes while they are being worn; they should always be taken off, however trivial the repair.

NEW CLOTHES

For those who could afford new clothes, there was a range of traditions which governed how and when they should be first worn.

For a start, it was important to avoid wearing new clothes for the first time on an unlucky day, such as Holy Innocents' Day (28 December), which was the unluckiest day of the year to do anything new, or any Friday (except Good Friday). If suitable, new clothes were best first worn to church on a Sunday. But the two times that were particularly favoured for new things were Easter and Whitsun. Samuel Pepys, writing in the seventeenth century, is one of many who recorded getting new clothes at Easter, but Whitsun was the preferred time for others, especially in the Midlands and north of England, where annual Whit walks and gatherings were immensely popular. The penalty for not wearing new clothes at the correct season was that 'the crows would "dirty" on you', but there were definite advantages in conforming to tradition:

At Whitsuntide every child (and most grown-ups too) had to have a new outfit. These Whitsuntide clothes were sacrosanct. Regardless of the size of the family, their social standing, or their income, come Whit Sunday morning all the children of the town donned their new finery and went from relation to relation; from friend to friend; from neighbour to neighbour, and on being visited the householder would give them a coin, maybe only a ha'penny, but as the morning progressed each child's pocket got heavier and heavier.

Sutton-in-Ashfield, Nottinghamshire

At other times, new clothes were a mixed blessing. There was a traditional saying with which kindly people would bless anyone seen wearing a new item for the first time – 'Health to wear it, strength to tear it and money to buy another' – but children had their own way of greeting a colleague sporting something new, which always involved pinching them hard: 'Pinch you for your new frock' was the phrase in Shropshire, and 'Nip for new, two for blue and three for corduroy!' was how the rhyme went in Victorian Yorkshire.

'HANDSELLING' NEW CLOTHES

Most superstitions relating to baby clothes generally matched the beliefs that surrounded adults' clothes, no doubt because it was thought that conditions at the beginning of life set the pattern for later on. This impulse led to the practice of 'handselling' new clothes by placing a small coin in the folds or pocket of the garment. To handsell meant to bring good fortune by ensuring a lucky beginning and was evident in many adult practices, including buying and selling, moving house, using a boat for the first time and so on. Indeed, superstitious people took great care over any situation which involved first use, even down to a baby's nappy:

In olden days two mutches [caps], an inner plain one and an outer one of more ornamental variety, were put on the child's head. The first inner one, taken off when soiled, was never washed and put on again, but flung in the fire. Similarly, the first soiled napkin was never washed and used again, but was flung out on the green.

This was noted in Kincardineshire in 1914, but it is often surprising how an apparently stray belief can crop up in different times and places. The idea of throwing the first nappy out in the open was already current in the 1760s, and in 1969 Iona Opie, author of the *Dictionary of Superstitions* (1989), was told by a Hampshire neighbour, 'Never wash the first nappy a baby dirties', although it is not made clear what one should do with it.

SEASONAL CLOTHING

Despite, or perhaps because of, our centrally heated houses and cars, the availability of a wide variety of fabrics for clothes, and all our other creature comforts, a constant worry for the modern parent is temperature – is the baby too hot, or too cold? In the past, the same worries were present but on a much simpler scale. We were all regularly exposed to the weather in all its uncertainty, and in winter our homes would routinely have the contrast of overheated kitchen/living rooms and freezing cold bedrooms, which had no heat at all except when someone was lying there sick. 'Ne'er cast a clout till May is out' has been a well-known proverb since at least the eighteenth century, and many parents followed it to the letter. In modern times it has been argued that the saying refers to the hawthorn plant (popularly called 'May') being 'out' or in bloom, but this is an interpretation with no foundation. It is perfectly clear from earlier versions that it is simply the month of May, not the plant, which was being invoked. Indeed, an alternative version declared, 'Till April is dead, change not a thread.'

There were many superstitions about the month of May, which reveal that it was seen in a very bad light, and was believed to be an uncanny time (see also p.52). For new parents, May was considered a bad time to make any alteration to their children's clothing, and in particular they were warned not to change babies out of their first, long gowns into shorter ones, a process often referred to as 'tucking': 'Tuck babies in May and you'll tuck them away' was a saying collected in Cornwall in 1887.

As far as clothing was concerned people often behaved as if there were only two seasons:

In some Norfolk villages, up to two or three years ago [mid-1920s], children were sewn into their clothes in the autumn, and these were not taken off till the spring.

Mollie Harris, remembering her Oxfordshire childhood in the same decade, noted:

Our winter salvation, apart from the great suet puddings we ate, was surely our 'possibles', a name we christened the flannel weskit we younger ones were annually sewn up in. Mother slapped goose-grease thickly on our backs and chests, then sewed us up in a piece of real flannel – next to the skin. This was kept on till spring! No proper baths were taken during the winter; we were merely topped and tailed – washed up as far as possible, and down as far as possible, 'possible' being that smelly greasy flannel weskit that was in such a state at the end of the winter that it was simply cut off our bodies and flung in the fire.

THE CORRECT WAY TO DRESS A BABY

It wasn't only what children wore that was subject to superstition, the method in which they were dressed was also important:

When an infant is first dressed, its clothes should never be put on over its head (which is very unlucky), but drawn over its feet.

This was recorded in County Durham in 1867, and the same was still being said in the 1980s, although no rational explanation has ever been suggested. The following example of the fear of tempting fate – often uppermost in parents' minds when their babies are small and particularly vulnerable – was recorded in Wales in 1909:

If you measure a child for garments in the first six months of its life, it will often want clothes.

Until little more than a century ago, young boys commonly wore dresses up to the age of five, and sometimes even later. Their hair was also kept long until well after the toddler stage, and in Victorian photographs of children at play it is often difficult to identify the sex of many of the younger ones. On closer inspection, however, it can be seen that boys' dresses tended to be more robust and without the frills and decorations sported by their sisters, and there was also a vast difference in the shape of their hats. Keeping boys in dresses was standard practice until the late nineteenth century, and lingered in many places well into the twentieth century. The day of a boy's transition to trousers or breeches, referred to as being 'breeched', was treated as something of a rite of passage and the occasion for family celebration.

PINK OR BLUE?

The idea that girls should be dressed in pink and boys in blue only surfaced in the 1920s, and did not become really standard practice until the 1930s. There does not seem to have been any agreed colour distinction before that time. Nevertheless, boys could still be finely attuned to other nuances of appropriate male attire at an early age. A member of the West Sussex Women's Institute, for example, remembering her own childhood in the area around the time of the First World War, described one such incident:

> My brothers and I wore woollen jerseys, the boys with corduroy shorts, I with pleated skirts. The jerseys were high-necked, buttoning across the shoulders, mine on the left and my brothers' on the right. When 'wearing thin' set in on the fronts and elbows, the garments were turned back to front to spread the wear. My brothers were wild with indignation because their buttons were now on the 'girls' side', apparently insulting their masculinity. My sister and I did not much like the change, but we did not protest. I am quite sure that my brothers would have preferred darned or even patched fronts and elbows to those hated girls'-side buttons.
>
> Sussex, 1914

Grand Old Duke of York

Oh the grand old Duke of York
He had ten thousand men,
He marched them up to the top of the hill
And he marched them down again.
And when they were up they were up,
And when they were down they were down,
And when they were only halfway up
They were neither up nor down.

There have been various attempts by amateur historians to pin down the exact Duke of York who is satirised in this rhyme, and the prime candidate is usually Frederick, who commanded the Flanders campaign in 1793. The fact that there were no hills anywhere near his army has not saved him from public ridicule every time a five-year-old sings the verse. But the Duke does not feature in this rhyme until the late nineteenth century, and previous versions featured other commanders, including Napoleon. The rhyme as we know it is merely a rewrite of an original verse which lampooned King Henri IV's military pretensions in 1610:

The King of France went up the hill
With forty thousand men,
The King of France came down the hill
And ne'er went up again.

or, in another version:

The King of France and forty thousand men
They drew their swords and put them up again.

The First Year

Hush-a-bye baby, on the tree top,
When the wind blows the cradle will rock,
When the bough breaks the cradle will fall,
Down will come baby, cradle and all.

Cradles and Prams

The cradle occupied a significant symbolic role in the household, which has now all but disappeared, although a few cradle beliefs have survived by being passed on to the pram. As the main symbol of babyhood, the cradle was surrounded by superstitious ideas which imbued it with an influence that would continue through the life of the child. So, for example, if the cradle was not paid for before the new baby arrived, the general belief was that the occupant would live a life of debt and in the end would not even have the money to pay for its own coffin. Nevertheless, the cradle's symbolic importance far outweighed its economic value, as in this comment from northern England in 1879:

> In all sales, either under distraint for rent or common debt, the cradle should be left unsold, and remain the property of its original owner.

NEW CRADLES

The question of newness exercised the mind of many a superstitious parent and there was a general prejudice against putting a baby into a brand new cradle:

> It is still considered unlucky by many to use a new cradle for a newborn infant. Old cradles are, therefore, in special request and are constantly borrowed to avoid the mysterious peril of using a new one.
>
> Fife, 1912

This runs contrary to the instincts of modern parents, who like to have all new things for their baby, but is part of a definite pattern of superstitions that reveal the fear of being 'the first' in many given situations. A regular motif that occurs in tales and beliefs of the past is the fear of being the first occupant of a new cemetery, or the first person to cross a new bridge, or even to live in a new house. In these contexts, the underlying fear was that the first person was claimed by the Devil as his due, and although there is no evidence that this was explicitly believed to be true of cradles, the pattern of thought is suggestively similar.

Nevertheless, the superstitious world is never simple, and there was another strong idea that inanimate objects such as cradles and prams could carry their own bad luck, and vestiges of this belief sometimes underlie the modern insistence on everything being new. Folklore writer Enid Porter noted such a case in 1961:

> A Cambridge woman . . . said that when her first baby, born in 1940, had died at the age of eighteen months she was sure that this was because she had bought a perambulator from a mother whose baby had lived for only three days.

In another context it is not the newness which matters, but the timing. Many modern parents are pleased to buy a new pram for their new baby, but refuse to have it delivered to the house before the baby arrives. Enid Porter again provides an example:

> 'We had the offer of a good second-hand pram,' said one Cambridge woman in 1961, 'but my husband said it would be tempting providence to buy one before the baby came, in case it didn't live to occupy it.'

This is a classic case of fear of 'tempting fate', and the idea is still quoted regularly in the twenty-first century.

ROCKING AN EMPTY CRADLE

This was seen as a form of tempting fate, though there is some disagreement about the particular danger involved in the action. An example from Highland Scotland, published in 1926, sums up the ambivalence:

There are two opposing beliefs regarding the rocking of an empty cradle. Some believe that:

> If you rock the cradle empty
> Then you shall have babies plenty

while others believe the exactly opposite, and others, again, believe that rocking the cradle thoughtlessly, as one may sometimes do, is an omen of the child's death.

But it should be said that the most commonly quoted result of rocking an empty cradle was, in England at least, that it brought a new baby in double-quick time. Another perspective takes a less drastic view, as recorded in Wales in 1909:

> If you rock an empty cradle, you will take the infant's rest away.

WOODEN CRADLES

There were numerous beliefs concerning the good or bad qualities of particular types of wood used to make a cradle, and one of the most common is a distrust of elder wood, as here from Lincolnshire:

> You must never have a baby's cot or cradle made with elder in it or your baby will get sick. It's the wood that's bad luck.

The elder is the tree which, by a large margin, is the most often named in traditional beliefs and practices in Britain, but in such diverse and contradictory manner that its true nature is impossible to pin down. It is often quoted, for example, as the tree on which Judas hanged himself, or the tree that provided the wood for the cross. It is lucky to have near the house because it is immune from lightning; it is unlucky to have near the house because witches love it; it must never be included in domestic firewood; its wood, berries, leaves and flowers are widely reported as essential ingredients in a range of traditional cures; and so on. The best that can be said for it is that it is 'uncanny' and should be handled with care.

CATS IN THE CRADLE

Until relatively recently, it was widely believed that cats might suffocate babies by lying across them when they are asleep:

> An inquest was held on Marie Page, an infant of four months, daughter of a costermonger, living in Harrow Street, Marylebone. On Sunday night the mother put the child to bed, and some time afterwards she found the cat lying across the infant's body. On removing the animal she found that the child was dead. Dr Rose stated that the death was caused by suffocation.
>
> *Daily News*, 15 December 1881

This was not regarded as an unusual and tragic accident, but a regular occurrence in homes with cats and babies. There was even sometimes a suggestion of deliberate action on the part of the cat, who out of jealousy wished to rid itself of an unwelcome rival, but others claimed that cats will simply find a nice warm place to sleep, and mean no harm. Either way, it is still said that cats should never be left alone in a room with a sleeping baby, nor should the child be left asleep in the pram out in the garden without a cover to prevent such a tragedy.

Previous generations had another angle on the same idea of the danger of suffocation, based on the idea that cats actually 'sucked the baby's breath away':

> A child of eighteen months old was found dead near Plymouth: and it appeared, on the coroner's inquest, that the child died in consequence of a cat sucking its breath, thereby occasioning a strangulation.
>
> *Annual Register*, 25 January 1791

It was even believed by many that cats' breath was actually poisonous to humans. This was taken for granted by Edward Topsell, for example, in his influential *History of Foure-Footed Beasts* (1607), which connects breath and hair:

> It is most certain that the breath and savour of cats consume the radical humour and destroy the lungs, and therefore they which keep their cats with them in their beds have the air corrupted and fall into fever hectics and

consumptions . . . When a child hath gotten the hair of a
cat into his mouth, it hath so cloven and stuck to the
place that it could not be got off again and hath in that
place bred either the wens [ulcers] or the king's evil
[scrofula]. To conclude this point it appeareth that this
cat is a dangerous beast.

Which brings us to witchcraft. One of the specific
reasons why cats were distrusted was their long-standing
association with witches, as their familiars and companions.
Less than a decade after Topsell's anti-feline piece, Ben
Jonson could have a 'hag' claim, in his *Masque of Queens*
(1616):

> Under a cradle I did creep
> By day; and when the child was asleep
> At night, I suck'd the breath; and rose
> And pluck'd the nodding nurse by the nose.

But even beyond the specifics of hair and suffocation, which
at least have some semblance of a factual basis, many people
claimed a more fundamental link between babies and cats –
especially kittens – that made it wise to keep the two as
separate as possible:

Several babies in this locality have recently been 'nash'
(i.e. in indifferent health). In every instance the household has included a kitten, and the mothers of babies

Lullabies

There are those who argue that the first songs ever sung by humans must have been hymns to some god or other, or perhaps the chants of men returning from a successful hunt. We will never know, but a much more likely candidate for the first ever musical utterance is the homely scene of a mother soothing her baby to sleep.

LULLING THE BABY TO SLEEP

For the youngest babies, it does not matter much what the song is about, as long as it has a regular rhythm and soothing tone, and it is likely that parents have always adapted popular songs of the day for the purpose. But there are also traditional patterns which last from generation to generation, and which everyone will instantly recognise as a lullaby, and these often have an interesting history. Each language, for example, seems to have particular words, or rather sounds, which crop up again and again in the context of soothing children. In English, the syllable 'lull' was one of these, which of course gives us the word 'lullaby'. One of the earliest known English examples, from the fifteenth century, runs:

> Lullay, myn lyking, my dere sone, myn swetying,
> Lullay, my dere herte, myn owyn dere delying.

In Scottish lullabies, 'baloo', 'ballaloo', and other similar sounds, are popular.

> No balloo, lammy, no balloo, my dear,
> Now balaloo, lammy, ain mammie is here.
> What ails my wee bairnie? What ails it this night?
> What ails my wee lammy? Is bairnie no right?

> Hush an baloo, babby
> Hush an baloo
> A the lave's in their beds [All the rest],
> I'm hushin you.

HUSH-A-BYE BABY

The syllable 'by' is popular in this language of sleep-inducing sounds, as in the word 'lullaby' itself, and in 'rock-a-bye', 'hush-a-bye' and even the term 'bye-byes', meaning 'sleep'. The most common example here is *Rock-a-bye baby* or *Hush-*

a-bye baby, which is probably the most widely known of all lullabies, being found all over the English-speaking world. It has changed little since its first known printing in *Mother Goose's Melody* (1765):

> Hush-a-bye baby, on the tree top,
> When the wind blows the cradle will rock,
> When the bough breaks the cradle will fall,
> Down will come baby, cradle and all.

But this book also included the didactic comment, 'This may serve as a warning to the proud and ambitious, who climb so high that they generally fall at last.' The central image of cradle and baby falling from a tree caused no problems for editors of illustrated nursery rhyme books of the past, who happily depicted both hurtling towards the ground. But sensibilities have changed, and modern books show much ingenuity in getting the precious bundle safely to earth. The cradle is shown descending gently on a giant leaf, or supported by four little birds each holding a ribbon in its beak, or even with the baby's blanket forming a parachute.

Another example of the 'rock-a-bye' format is the following, first noted in 1805:

> Rock-a-bye baby,
> Thy cradle is green,
> Father's a nobleman,
> Mother's a queen,

And Betty's a lady
And wears a gold ring,
And Johnny's a drummer
And drums for the king.

These words have more of a fairytale quality, which must
have contrasted strangely with many a poor cottage interior.
A little more down-to-earth is this one collected in
Cambridgeshire in 1914:

Sleep like a lady (or gentleman),
You shall have milk
When the cows come home.
Father is a butcher,
Mother cooks the meat,
Johnnie rocks the cradle
While baby goes to sleep.

BABY BUNTING

Another well-known lullaby, again not changed much since
its first appearance in 1784, is *Bye baby bunting*:

Bye baby bunting,
Daddy's gone a-hunting,
Gone to get a rabbit's skin
To wrap the baby bunting in.

'Bunting' is an old term of endearment – probably meaning short and plump. A Scottish version runs:

> Hushie ba, burdie beeton,
> Your mammie's gane to Seaton,
> For to buy a lammie's skin
> To wrap your bonnie boukie in.

Childhood Illnesses

Modern medicine has eliminated many of the illnesses that formerly were viewed as almost routine setbacks to be endured by the majority of infants in their first year. Most created greater or lesser degrees of discomfort for a few days, though others might carry with them more serious threats of permanent disability or even death. It is no surprise that superstition provided a catalogue of advice and cures to which worried parents might have recourse.

Many of us have a romantic idea of the past when it comes to home doctoring. We like to think of Granny collecting herbs and making up medicines to recipes passed down through the generations, from a time when our ancestors were in tune with nature and possessed a folk knowledge that we have somehow lost in our scientific age. But the reality, before the early twentieth century, was very different. While some herbs could indeed alleviate symptoms and certain people were expert in, say, the setting of broken bones, everyone was equally ignorant of anatomy, hygiene, diet, germ theory and how diseases were caused and spread. In many cases the treatment was more dangerous than the condition. Amateur village doctoring was a colourful hotch-potch of herbs, patent medicines, charms, magical cures, superstition and faith, and was often vividly recalled in people's autobiographies as a part of everyday life, something that has changed beyond recognition. Don Haworth, for example, remembering his childhood in Lancashire in the 1930s, recorded:

My grandmother had a religious belief that there was a herb in the field to cure every malady, which benefice was evidenced by the invariable growth of healing docks close to stinging nettles. If you pointed to the columns of the week's departed in the paper, or to Jack Yates at his wits' end in February to get enough coffins knocked up to maintain the Co-op's funeral service, she would repeat that the herbs existed but remained to be discovered.

PROBLEMS WITH BREATHING

Respiratory problems were a direct result of damp, over-crowded living conditions and were particularly widespread. One of the key principles in their treatment was the idea that they could be cured by getting the patient to breathe in certain pungent smells, or the air from particular places. Industrial smells, such as those emanating from a gasworks or from hot tar were particularly valued in this respect, as recalled by a WI member in *Lancashire Within Living Memory* (1993):

> One day when I was little we were going to the greengrocer's, my mother and I, and we passed a group of men retarring the stone sets in the road. There was a large horse and waggon and in the road stood a vat of hot liquid. Mother stopped and had a word with the men. Then, to my consternation, she lifted me up in her arms and held me so that my head was over the vat. 'Breathe in, love, it will help to cure your cold,' she said. I cannot remember whether I obeyed or not. I was too terrified she would drop me into the cauldron.

But there were also particular places or situations that were reputed to be effective in this respect: the summit of certain local hills, ferry boats, trains going through particular tunnels, and so on. Animals also played a part in these cures. There are reports of children being carried round a flock of sheep and encouraged to breathe in the air. Other creatures had a more direct use.

> Wisha, Peig, if ye had any white gander at home and put him under a creel till morning; and then if you opened the little boy's mouth and let the gander breathe down

well into his throat, I guarantee you there wouldn't be a
trace of the disease left in your little boy.

Great Blasket Island, Southwest Ireland, 1908

WHOOPING COUGH

There was a widespread and magical cure for whooping
cough which involved a donkey. It was a widely held belief
that following his triumphal entry into Jerusalem Jesus had
blessed the donkey, a idea corroborated by the black marks on
the beast's back which were often thought to be in the shape
of a cross.

> The old people had a cure for the chincough. The child
> with the chincough was put over and under a donkey
> three times. Two people did that, one handing the child
> over to the other. The donkey would sometimes get
> oaten meal to eat, and the child would get a fingerful of
> what the donkey had left. They say that there is a
> blessing on a donkey on account of the cross it has on its
> back.

County Donegal, 1864

It was even said that, because of this cross, the donkey was the
only animal shape which the Devil could not assume. Various
parts of the donkey could be used as amulets:

The Rev. S. Rundle, vicar of Godolphin [Cornwall], says, 'That once he was sent for to baptise a child, around whose neck hung a little bag, which the mother said contained a bit of a donkey's ear, and that this charm had cured the child of a most distressing cough.

While the application of herbs and other natural remedies may or may not be scientifically sound, these donkey cures reside in the realm of pure magical thinking, and there were at least as many magical cures as there were herbal ones.

MINOR AILMENTS

All minor childhood ailments, such as toothache, earache, chilblains and so on, were combated with a legion of cures and preventative measures. Beating chilblains with holly was one widely recommended cure, and there were ways to prevent them forming in the first place:

Hardening of infants: As a means of hardening a newborn infant it is thought to be a sure preventative against chilblains for its feet to be put in the snow.

Dorset, 1912

Spiders, alive or dead, were swallowed to counter fevers, and cuts were liberally plastered with cobwebs, the thicker and blacker the better, to stop the bleeding. Earache was treated with various items, always heated and placed in or on the ear, including a small onion, the juice of eels rendered down or a sock full of salt. There were enough methods of getting rid of warts, ranging from the pseudo-medical to the overtly magical, to fill a large volume on their own, and some people still believe that they can be 'bought' by another person offering a small sum of money to the sufferer.

THE BENEFIT OF AMULETS

Wearing certain things round the neck or waist was long considered useful as a preventative measure or cure against childhood illnesses. The Oxfordshire diarist Mollie Harris noted in the 1920s:

> Our next-door neighbour's daughter was supposed to be 'weak in the chest', and she was never seen without her 'velvety band' as her mother called it. It was a narrow, black velvet band fastened tightly round her neck, and this was only taken off when she washed. She wore this well into her teens and for all I know she may be still wearing one.

A similar line of thought was revealed in the early years of the twentieth century when it was discovered that many working-class children in London, and elsewhere, wore necklaces of blue beads to combat bronchitis and other chest infections. These necklaces were placed around a baby's neck, and they were never again without one for the rest of their childhood.

There seems to have been no end of things which could be worn in this way. Don Haworth from Lancashire recorded in the 1930s:

> We wore a sachet of camphor on a string round our neck and were dosed after meals with cod liver oil and malt. Refinements developed, the camphor bag was replaced by an 'iodine locket', a tiny tin case which was claimed to house a powerful general prophylactic. The cod liver oil and malt was superseded by proprietary sugar-coated pills, said to contain 'concentrate'. They cost money that should have gone on food. Nobody was to know.

If the eel and spider cures seem strange to modern eyes, there were others which were even more bizarre. For centuries it was widely believed that if a wound was caused by a knife or other metal object, it would not heal if the knife was allowed to get dirty or go rusty. Many people put more energy into keeping the knife clean than the wound it had caused, and many a rusty nail has been polished back to brightness after someone has stepped on it.

Another long-standing misconception about health was the idea of a direct connection between the feet and the rest of the body. For centuries, the standard last-ditch cure for a severe fever was to cut a live pigeon in half and apply the bird's body to the soles of the patient's feet, in hopes of drawing the fever out. This was not an obscure and unusual treatment, but was standard practice – from the lowliest cottage to the deathbeds of royalty. The pigeon treatment lasted in isolated cases until the turn of the twentieth century, but the importance of the feet lingered on for many more years. Don Haworth wrote of his childhood:

> The crucial area to keep dry, we learned, was the feet because the blood went straight from them to the heart, which would run rough like a cold engine. In fact few children suffered from wet feet because some had wellingtons and the clogs worn by the rest were less vulnerable to deterioration than shoes.

Supernatural Threats

In the superstitious world of the past, the threat from malevolent forces was a constant presence, but there were certain key times when that danger was markedly increased. Weddings and funerals were two of those times when extra care needed to be taken, but childbirth and the baby's first months in the world were the most dangerous time of all. From the moment of birth, the baby was believed to be in grave danger of harm from ill-wishers, both human and supernatural, at least until baptism, and the mother was similarly at risk until she had been churched. It is hard today to comprehend how seriously the idea of supernatural threats to mother and baby were taken in the past, and the lengths to which people would go to ensure protection.

FAIRIES AND CHANGELINGS

Fairies were suspected of causing all kinds of mischief, but by far the most worrying thing that they were accused of doing was taking a human baby and replacing it with one of their own – a changeling. The archetypal changeling was like a grotesque parody of a baby: it screamed and cried constantly, ate voraciously but did not thrive, never progressed mentally or physically and showed no affection for its poor human parents.

It is clear now that the notion of the changeling was invented to explain congenital diseases and disabilities from which some unfortunate infants suffered and which were then far more common than now. It is hardly surprising that many parents believed that supernatural forces were at work. The following tale was recorded by Lady Wilde in her collection *Ancient Legends, Mystic Charms and Superstitions of Ireland* (1888):

> A woman in County Galway had a beautiful child, so handsome, that all the neighbours were very careful to say 'God bless it' when they saw him, for they knew the fairies would desire to steal the child, and carry it off to the hills.
>
> But one day it chanced that an old woman, a stranger, came in. 'Let me rest,' she said, 'for I am weary.' And she sat down and looked at the child, but never said, 'God bless it.' And when she had rested, she rose up, looked again at the child fixedly, in silence, and then went her way.

All that night the child cried and would not sleep.
And all next day it moaned as if in pain. So the mother
told the priest, but he would do nothing for fear of the
fairies. And just as the poor mother was in despair, she
saw a strange woman going by the door. 'Who knows,'
she said to her husband, 'but this woman would help
us.' So they asked her to come in and rest. And when
she looked at the child she said 'God bless it' instantly,
and spat three times at it, and then sat down. 'Now what
will you give me,' she said, 'if I tell you what ails the
child?' 'I will cross your hand with silver,' said the
mother, 'as much as you want, only speak,' and she laid
the money on the woman's hand. 'Now tell me the
truth, for the sake and in the name of Mary, and the
good Angels.'

'Well,' said the stranger, 'the fairies have had your
child these two days in the hills, and this is a
changeling they have left in its place. But so many
blessings were said on your child that the fairies can do
it no harm. For there was only one blessing wanting,
and only one person gave the Evil Eye. Now you must
watch for this woman, carry her into the house, and
secretly cut off a piece of her cloak. Then burn the
piece close to the child, till the smoke as it rises makes
him sneeze; and when this happens the spell is broken,
and your own child will come back to you safe and
sound, in place of the changeling.' Then the stranger
rose up and went her way.

All that evening the mother watched for the old woman, and at last she spied her on the road. 'Come in,' she cried, 'come in, good woman, and rest, for the cakes are hot on the griddle, and supper is ready.' So the woman came in, but never said 'God bless you kindly' to man or mortal, only scowled at the child, who cried worse than ever. Now the mother had told her eldest child to cut off a piece of the old woman's cloak, when she sat down to eat. And the girl did as she was desired, and handed the piece to her mother, unknown to anyone. But, to their surprise, this was no sooner done than the woman rose up and went out without uttering a word; and they saw her no more. Then the father carried the child outside, and burned the piece of cloth before the door, and held the boy over the smoke till he sneezed three times violently; after which he gave the child back to the mother, who laid him in his bed, where he slept peacefully, with a smile on his face, and cried no more with the cry of pain. And when he woke up the mother knew that she had got her own darling child back from the fairies, and no evil thing happened to him any more.

In some stories, however, the changeling was tricked into revealing his true nature. In many cases this was simply by making ostentatious preparations for the traditional ordeals by fire or exposure, which the changeling observes and then decides to get out while he can. In another, more humorous, vein, the fairy is tricked into revealing himself. Playing on the idea that changelings often look like young humans but are really very very old, a widespread tale tells of one being given a set of pipes, on which he cannot resist showing off his skill. In another, the fairy is confronted with an elaborate play-acted scene in which the housewife declares she must make breakfast for all the farmworkers and mixes a tiny quantity of oatmeal and milk in an eggshell which is placed over the fire. Changelings normally do not speak, but this one cries out in astonishment, 'I have lived long enough to see yonder wood grow up and die three times, but I have never seen porridge made in an eggshell before.'

Changeling stories and beliefs were found in most European countries, and have been recorded in all parts of Britain and Ireland, although markedly less often in England than in Scotland, Ireland and Wales, primarily because in England the active fairy tradition began to lose its power earlier than elsewhere. Changeling beliefs lingered longest where fairy beliefs still held sway and, broadly speaking, these were the places that remained rural until a relatively late time.

WITCHCRAFT

The story told by Lady Wilde, given above, conflates the two main culprits in these matters – witches and fairies – although these are more usually kept separate. According to popular belief, witches did not normally replace babies with surrogates, or work in league with the fairies, but could cause the baby to pine away and die by using their malevolent arts.

'Overlooking', or inflicting the baleful influence of the 'evil eye', was just one way in which a witch might bring harm to a baby. Belief in such powers ran very deep in rural societies, and was the basis for countless accusations of witchcraft:

Several examples are recorded of men and women in the island who had the power of the evil eye. The power was so strong that if, when milking, they but glanced at the milk in the pail, it would turn sour before it reached the dairy. If a witch had a grudge against a farmer's wife and should cast her evil eye on the churn, when churning was in progress, no butter would come; a fact known to me.

Jersey, 1914

The Irish are very susceptible to omens. They say, 'Beware of a childless woman who looks fixedly at your child.'

Ireland, 1888

Applying the influence of the evil eye could be done quite simply, and even accidentally, as in this report published in *Notes & Queries* in 1868:

One day Mrs R.'s nurse happened to meet Mrs E.'s in a shop, with 'the baby', and as nurses do, she kissed the child, and praised its good looks, healthy appearance, etc., but unfortunately forgot to say 'God bless it', or to make the gesture of spitting on the child. Almost immediately on the child being brought home it was seized with an attack of convulsions, which after some time proved fatal. The child lived till the next day, and its distracted mother, having heard of the occurrence in the shop, sent off to Mrs R. to beg that the nurse should be sent to her house . . . [She was] deeply grieved at what she supposed had happened through her forgetfulness . . . She blessed the child three times, and spat upon it, but all in vain; the child soon after expired, and both mother and nurse were perfectly convinced that its death was entirely owing to the latter having, however unintentionally, 'overlooked' it by omitting the proper ceremonies when praising it.

COUNTER-SPELLS AND CHARMS
TO PROTECT THE BABY

In addition to saying words of blessing and carrying out counter-spells, there were many other ways of protecting the mother and newborn baby from witches and other malefactors. Various symbolic items could be placed in or around the cradle – Bibles, of course, but also knives or other objects made of iron, pieces of rowan or mountain ash, and so on:

A person was invariably appointed for [the baby's] special protection, and when she had occasion to leave the child in its cradle she would place the tongs, which must be made of iron, across it till her return. Another specific to ward off evil from babies was to put salt in their mouths as soon as possible after their birth.

Isle of Man, 1891

A necklace of coral beads kept witchcraft at bay (see p.176), or one could buy special brooches:

My first experience of witchcraft began at a very early age, before I was an hour old, in fact. My maternal grandmother, a pure-bred Highlander, held me close to the fire and, taking care that she was unobserved, quietly fastened this witch-brooch beneath the ample skirts of my baby-garments. This form of brooch, fastened in the manner above described, was firmly believed to possess the power of driving the witches, which lay in wait for all newly born children, up the chimney. It protected the wearer from their malevolence, and brought good luck. The rite was practised universally in rural districts throughout the north in my grandmother's time. My mother probably had some germs of scepticism in her mind, but considered that her darling would be safer if the charm were applied in the orthodox manner. Amongst the fishing population this superstition lingered till a much later date; jewellers in Aberdeen had to give fishermen's brides a witch-brooch, along with the wedding-ring, up to about thirty years ago. It was first worn by the bride to bring good luck to the household.

Scotland, 1896

Brooches like these were very popular in Scotland, and else-where, from about the seventeenth century, and were called either 'witch brooches' or 'luckenbooth brooches', after the 'lock-up' booths in Edinburgh's Mile End, where they were typically sold. The brooches varied enormously in price and quality, with something to suit every pocket, and at the top end of the market were made of silver or gold and encrusted with gems. The basic shape was an open-work asymmetrical heart, sometimes with a crown on top. More recent examples often represented two hearts entwined, to accentuate the wedding gift angle at the expense of the brooch's baby-protection attributes.

One recurrent feature in reports of protection against fairies and witches is that items belonging to the father of the baby are powerful in this respect, as in this piece published in 1879:

In Scotland the little one's safeguard is held to lie in the juxtaposition of some article of dress belonging to the father. This was experienced by the wife of a shepherd near Selkirk. Soon after the birth of her first child, a fine boy, she was lying in bed with her baby by her side, when suddenly she became aware of a confused noise of talking and merry laughter in the 'spence', or room. This, in fact, proceeded from the fairies, who were forming a child of wax as a substitute for the baby, which they were planning to steal away. The poor mother expected as much, so in great alarm she seized her husband's waistcoat, which chanced to be lying at the foot of the bed, and flung it over herself and the child. The fairies set up a loud scream, calling out, 'Auld Luckie has cheated us o' our bairnie.' Soon afterwards, the woman heard something fall down the lum (or chimney) and looking out she saw a waxen image of her baby, stuck full of pins, lying on the hearth. When her husband came home he made up a large fire and threw the fairy lump upon it; but, instead of burning, the thing flew up the chimney, and the house instantly resounded with shouts of joy and peals of laughter.

Teeth

Teeth loom large in the superstitions of babies and childcare. It is perhaps understandable that traditions would cluster around the baby's teething process – a painful and distressing time for all concerned – but as is usual in the realm of superstition, the remedies are more often symbolic and magical than genuinely therapeutic.

NECKLACES TO COMBAT TEETHING PAIN

There is a very long tradition of things being worn round the necks of babies to help them through their teething, but the items concerned have varied considerably. The substance with the longest history in this respect is coral, which was recorded by the Latin writer Pliny, as early as AD 77, as having the power to protect the wearer from danger and witchcraft. It is not known why coral was imbued with these protective properties, but its power was widely believed and was often mentioned by British writers from at least the sixteenth century onwards. Many specifically mention the protection of children, and Thomas Browne, in his influential collection *Pseudodoxia Epidemica*, first published in 1646, specifically connects the coral necklace with teething:

> Though coral doth properly preserve and fasten the teeth in men, yet it is used in children to make an easier passage for them and for that intent is worn about their necks.

Coral was the most widely reported material used for necklaces, but other substances were also used, including dried deadly nightshade berries in Norfolk. Some children wore a little bag fastened on a string round the neck, in which were kept woodlice and donkey hairs, among other items. The maverick folklorist Edward Lovett (1852–1933), who was a bank clerk by day and an obsessive collector of trifles at weekends, recorded the wearing of real teeth in working-class districts of London:

> If a young girl 'lost' a tooth (i.e. it came out) she put it away very carefully so that in the event of her marrying and having children she would hang the tooth round the neck of the child during the period of cutting its teeth . . . One Saturday night, about 1905, I was in a poor man's market in South London, when I saw upon a hawker's

barrow a small card box containing a couple of calf's teeth. I asked the man in charge what they were for, and his answer was: 'You wouldn't believe me if I told you.' To this I replied that I knew already what he would tell me, and that I would give him sixpence for them. He was quite pleased with this, and, having completed the deal, he said, 'And what do you think you're going to do with 'em?' I told him that they would be put in a little bag and tied round the neck of a baby that was cutting its first teeth with difficulty. He seemed very surprised that I should have heard of this.

RUBBING THE GUMS

Teething problems could be tackled more directly, by rubbing substances on the gums, as reported in Guernsey in 1975:

Gums through which the teeth are showing, but having difficulty to come through, should be rubbed with a wedding ring.

The key point here is that to be effective it is a gold ring that is required, and the same procedure was widely recommended for dealing with a sty on the eye, and other such ailments.

Much more elaborate ceremonies were also devised, such as this one recorded in northeastern Scotland in the 1870s:

On the first symptoms of the child's cutting teeth, a 'teethin bannock' was made. It was baked of oatmeal and butter or cream, sometimes with the addition of a ring, in presence of a few neighbours, and without a single word being spoken by the one baking it. When prepared, it was given to the child to play with till it was broken. A small piece was then put into the child's mouth, if it had not done so of its own accord. Each one present carried away a small portion. Such a bannock was supposed to ease the troubles of teething. It went also by the name of 'teethiny plaster'.

FIRST TOOTH

The appearance of a baby's first teeth allowed plenty of material for prophecies about the baby's future life and character. Long before the Tooth Fairy was invented there were widespread worries about what to do with milk teeth when they were shed, and elaborate rituals which governed their disposal. It was particularly important to take note of where the baby's first tooth appeared, as a correspondent to *Notes & Queries* reports:

A Rutland woman was telling me [in 1878] that her baby had just cut his first tooth, but that she was sorry to say it was in his upper jaw. I said I supposed it did not make much difference whether it was in the upper or lower jaw. She replied that it made all the difference in the world, as if it was in the upper jaw it was a sign that the child would not live.

The undesirability of a top tooth was widely acknowledged, and an early death was prophesied, although in Scotland an alternative reading was that it meant the child would never be married. On a more positive note, a 'bottom tooth' was welcomed, as recorded in Derbyshire in 1891:

> A baby in which I have an interest was found to have cut its first tooth the other day. It was a bottom tooth, and the servant exclaimed, 'A long life! A long life!' It is here considered lucky for a baby to cut a bottom tooth first.

Occasionally, a baby is born with a tooth already in place, and it was generally agreed that this must be strongly indicative of the child's future character, but in the recorded examples there is little agreement as to the precise meaning. On the one hand it could be one of the worst of signs:

> It is very unlucky to be born with a tooth. Richard III was and his nephews said to him: 'Uncle, how ugly you are! You have a hump on your back, and they say you had teeth when you were born.' For this speech Richard became the boys' enemy, and revenged himself upon them after their father's death. So said Mrs Dudley.
>
> Shropshire, 1883

To be born with teeth is an extremely bad sign. The usual theory is that it foretells death by violence, but one midwife informed me a few years ago that the true meaning is even worse. 'I never speak of it,' she said, 'and if anyone asks me I deny it, for the sake of the mother; but it means that the child will grow up to be a murderer.'

Gloucestershire, 1951

Others maintained a completely opposite stance, in the fishing communities of Fife, in 1912, for example:

It occasionally happens that a child is born with one or more of its teeth cut. This is considered very lucky.

And in Denbighshire in 1930:

A child born with a tooth will become notable, and widely separated teeth denote that the owner will travel far from his native place.

Either way, most mothers dreaded early teething, because there was a widespread saying, 'Soon teeth, soon toes', which predicted that the next baby would follow quickly afterwards.

DISPOSING OF MILK TEETH

It may come as a surprise to many modern parents that the Tooth Fairy is a very recent invention, imported to Britain in the 1960s, probably from America. Before that time, there were a number of customary procedures which had to be followed when a child shed a tooth, but by far the most common was to sprinkle the tooth with salt and throw it on the fire:

> Milk-teeth are still commonly burnt as they fall out. This is not now done as a protection against witchcraft but because, as one young urban mother recently remarked, 'it would be very unlucky to lose the tooth, so it is better to burn it' . . . A teacher in an Oxfordshire school reported that if one of her pupils sheds a tooth during school-hours, he or she will never allow it to be burnt then and there. It must be taken home for the mother to throw on the kitchen fire. To let anyone else perform the rite would be both improper and foolish.
>
> Oxfordshire, 1957

Apart from the fear of witchcraft, the main concern in the disposal of a shed tooth was that if the correct procedures were not carried out, the replacement would be deformed:

> The child must be careful in disposing of its milk teeth as they fall out, and is often told to put salt on them and burn them. If a dog were to swallow one, the new tooth

would be like a dog's; if a pig ate it, it would be like a
pig's; and so on with other animals

Jersey, 1927

From about the 1920s, some people began to say that the
fairies took away any lost teeth (leaving a coin in lieu), and
this explanation gradually gained ground against the salt and
fire method, until the rapid spread of the now ubiquitous
Tooth Fairy.

Another strong reason for not leaving shed teeth lying
around was the idea that everyone has to account for their
teeth (and any other removed body parts) at the Day of
Judgement:

> The other day I saw a person throw her tooth, which had
> just been extracted, into the fire. I asked why she did
> this, and was told, 'That I shall not have to look for it
> when I die'
>
> Lancashire, 1870

I always heard, when a child, that the penalty for not
throwing teeth into the fire was general ill-luck, and also
that one's ghost would have to return and look for them.
This dwells in my memory the more, for having once
helped in a search, frantic but fruitless, for the dropped
tooth of a little cousin, lost in a ploughed field at twilight.

1870

GAPS IN TEETH

Once the teeth had grown, there were numerous other beliefs which came into play, such as the fact that a gap between the front teeth was a lucky sign, as recorded in Wales in 1930:

> The old women say: 'Watch well when the child has finished cutting its first teeth, for if there is a parting between the two front teeth to admit the passing of a sixpenny-piece, that individual will have riches and prosperity all through life.'

Oranges and Lemons

Oranges and lemons
Say the bells of St Clement's.
You owe me five farthings
Say the bells of St Martin's.
When will you pay me?
Say the bells of Old Bailey.
When I grow rich
Say the bells of Shoreditch.
When will that be?
Say the bells of Stepney.
I do not know
Says the great bell of Bow.

This rhyme on the churches of central London, despite taking considerable liberties with both rhyme and metre to make the names fit, is extremely well known, and has been popular for at least 250 years, although the words have changed considerably in that time. The earliest version, of about 1744, starts with these words:

Two sticks and an apple
Ring ye bells at Whitechapel.
Old Father Bald Pate
Ring ye bells at Aldgate.
Maids in white aprons
Ring ye bells at St Catherine's

and then continues with the 'oranges and lemons', the last two lines being

When I am old
Ring ye bells at St Paul's.

Although the 'oranges and lemons' version has now become standard, it was not uncommon in the past for people to make rhymes on their local churches, but the lines are always dictated by the particular names in the locality, such as:

Pancakes and fritters
Say All Saints and St Peter's

or

O very well
Says little Michael.

Index